Deserts of the World

MARY JO NICKUM

Aquitaine Ltd
Phoenix, Arizona

Deserts of the World

MARY JO NICKUM

Aquitaine Ltd
Phoenix, Arizona

Copyright © 2023 Mary Jo Nickum

Printed in the United States of America

All Rights Reserved

No part of this book may be used or reproduced by any means, graphic, electronic, or mechanical, including photocopying, recording, taping or by any information storage retrieval system without the written permission of the publisher, except in the case of brief quotations embodied in articles and reviews.

Reviewers may quote passages for use in periodicals, newspapers, or broadcasts provided credit is given to *Deserts of the World* by Mary Jo Nickum and Aquitaine, Ltd.

Aquitaine, LTD)

ISBN: 9781736467213

Library of Congress Cataloging Number LCCN: 2023947961

Printed in the United States of America

First Edition

DEDICATION

This book is dedicated to young people everywhere who

Don't like to or find it difficult to read and

Who, therefore, live on the fringes of a happy, healthy life.

Learn to enjoy reading and the world can be yours.

Believe in yourselves

Table of Contents

I. What Is a Desert? 1
   Deserts 3
   Desert Location in Relation to Atmosphere 5
   Desert Distribution 7

II. How Deserts Are Formed 9
   Climate 10
   Geography 13
   Desertification 16
   How can desertification be reduced? 18

III. Major Deserts of the World 20
   Deserts of Antarctica 25
   Deserts of Africa 27
   Deserts of the Americas 42
   The Deserts of South America 51
   Deserts of Asia 56
   Deserts of Australia 74

IV. Plants and Animals in the Desert 84
   Desert Animals 94

V. Peoples of the Desert	109
Berbers of North Africa	110
The Bedouins	116
The Bejas	118
The Sāns	120
Australian Aborigines	122
Natives of the North American Deserts	125
VI. Future of the Desert	139
Glossary	143
Side Bars	146
List of Illustrations	148
Illustration Credits	151
Sources	155
About the Author	160

The Arabian Desert

I. What Is a Desert?

Deserts are areas that receive very little precipitation. People often use the adjectives 'hot', 'dry', and 'empty' to describe deserts but these words do not tell the whole story. Although some deserts are extremely hot, with daytime temperatures as high as 130 degrees F, other deserts have cold winters or are cold year-round and most deserts, far from being empty and lifeless, are home to a variety of plants, animals, and other organisms. People have adapted to life in the desert for thousands of years.

One thing all deserts have in common is they are arid, or dry. Most experts agree a desert is an area of land receiving no more than 10 inches of precipitation a year. The amount of evaporation in a desert often greatly exceeds the annual rainfall. In all deserts, there is little water available for plants and other organisms.

Deserts are found on every continent and cover about one-fifth of Earth's land area **(Side Bar A)**. They are home to around 1 billion people—one-sixth of the Earth's population.

Although the word 'desert' may bring to mind a sea of shifting sand, dunes cover only about 10 percent of the world's deserts. Some deserts are mountainous. Others are dry expanses of rock, sand, or salt flats.

Side Bar A: Major Deserts of the World

Name	Type of Desert	Surface Area	Location
Antarctic	Polar	5.5 million mi^2	Antarctica
Arctic	Polar	5.4 million mi^2	Alaska, Canada, Greenland, Iceland, Norway, Sweden, Finland, Russia
Sahara	Subtropical	3.5 million mi^2	Northern Africa
Arabian	Subtropical	1 million mi^2	Arabian Peninsula
Gobi	Cold Winter	500,000 mi^2	China and Mongolia
Patagonian	Cold Winter	260,000 mi^2	Argentina
Great Victoria	Subtropical	250,000 mi^2	Australia
Kalahari	Subtropical	220,000 mi^2	South Africa, Botswana, Namibia
Great Basin	Cold Winter	190,000 mi^2	United States
Syrian	Subtropical	190,000 mi^2	Syria, Iraq, Jordan, Saudi Arabia
Chihuahuan	Subtropical	175,000 mi^2	Mexico
Great Sandy	Subtropical	150,000 mi^2	Australia
Kara-Kum	Cold Winter	135,000 mi^2	Uzbekistan, Turkmenistan
Colorado Plateau	Cold Winter	130,000 mi^2	United States
Gibson	Subtropical	120,000 mi^2	Australia
Sonoran	Subtropical	120,000 mi^2	United States, Mexico
Kyzyl-Kum	Cold Winter	115,000 mi^2	Uzbekistan, Turkmenistan, Kazakhstan
Takla Makan	Cold Winter	105,000 mi^2	China
Iranian	Cold Winter	100,000 mi^2	Iran
Thar	Subtropical	75,000 mi^2	India, Pakistan
Simpson	Subtropical	56,000 mi^2	Australia
Mojave	Subtropical	54,000 mi^2	United States
Atacama	Cool Coastal	54,000 mi^2	Chile
Namib	Cool Coastal	13,000 mi^2	Angola, Namibia, South Africa

Deserts

Think about all of the different types of habitats you have been to or have seen on television. The earth is covered in many different types of habitats that vary by climate and by the animals and plants that live there.

One unique type of habitat is a desert. **Deserts** are defined as regions with low rainfall, usually less than 10 inches of rain per year. Because of limited rainfall, deserts often have extraordinarily dry soil or sand that is easily moved around by wind. This results in a continuously changing landscape.

Although deserts are characteristically dry, in some regions, when it rains, it pours. In many desert regions, it will rain once or twice per year but will dump more than 5 inches of rain in a short time period. The landscape cannot absorb the large amount of rain and the result is often a flash flood, when large quantities of water flow over the land for a short period of time.

Another distinct characteristic of deserts is the unique organisms and plants that live there. Although at first glimpse a desert may look sparse or abandoned, there is actually a great deal of life present. There are many specialized plants that have developed adaptations, making it possible for them to live in such a harsh and dry climate. These plants survive by storing water in large root systems and by having small, waxy leaves to reduce water loss. A cactus is a prime example of a desert plant that has adapted to life with limited water. There are even some plants in the desert that look dead for most of the year but will become green and flower when it rains.

There also are many animals living in desert habitats. Similar to plants, these animals have developed adaptations to help them survive. Many desert organisms live in deep, cool burrows underground. They use these burrows to avoid the heat and some even hibernate in the ground during periods of extreme drought. Some desert animals are only active at night when it's cooler. Camels survive life in the desert by drinking large amounts of water when it is available and storing it in their body for later use. Because of this adaptation, some camels can survive for weeks without drinking.

Desert Location in Relation to Atmosphere

The location of deserts is directly related to the **atmosphere**. The **hydrosphere** also is involved in the creation of deserts. Water from the hydrosphere evaporates and travels into the atmosphere. The air above oceans and lakes is often very moist because of the large amount of water in the air. The atmosphere can cause the air and water particles to move around the globe.

The global pattern of air circulation controls where air moves around the planet. If the moist air travels over land near the equator, it will rise, expand and cool, which causes precipitation. Because of the large volume of precipitation that occurs, the air becomes dry as it travels north or south of the equator. This air will later sink, compress and warm and will not be able to form precipitation over the land. Additionally, the dry air will cause increased evaporation, contributing to the formation of a desert. When the amount of evaporation is greater than the amount of precipitation then a desert is formed.

Between the Tropic of Cancer to the Tropic of Capricorn **(Side Bar B)**, easterly wind enters in any continent by its eastern side. At the time of entry, they have sufficient amount of **moisture content** but when it reaches over the land surface water vapor easily evaporates and converts into dryer air and the amount of dryness of air is increased when the air move toward the west from the east. When it reaches the western part then it does not have sufficient amount of water vapor for precipitation. So, there is less amount of rainfall to occur.

Side Bar B Wind Direction

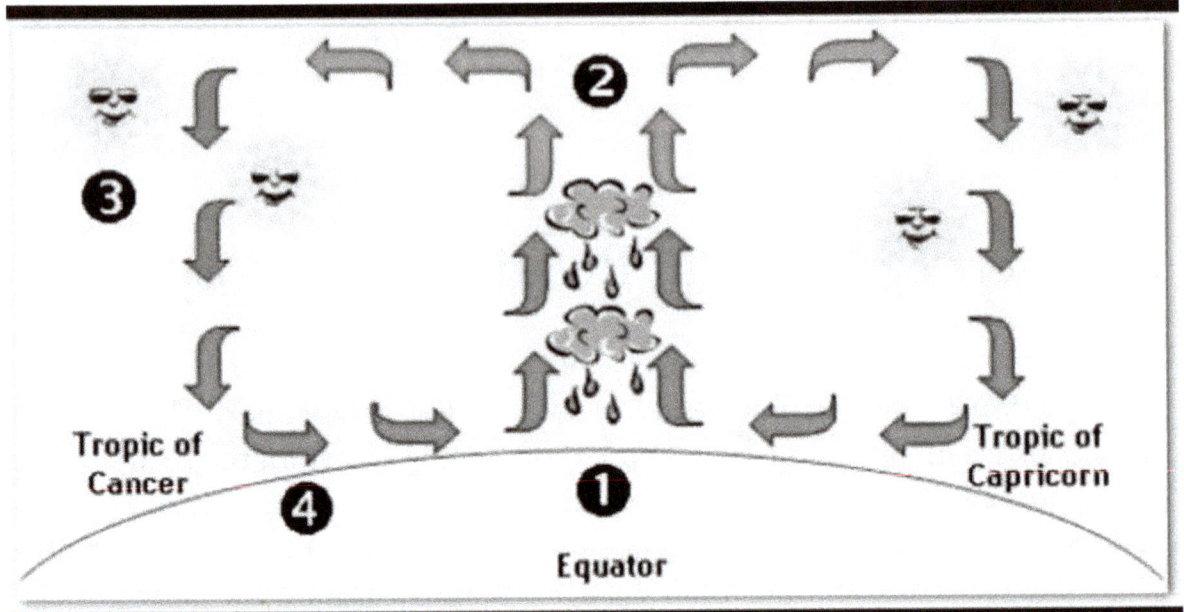

Desert Distribution

Because of the global pattern of air circulation and the relation to the atmosphere, most deserts are found within a belt centered on the 30° North and 30° South latitude (the Tropical Belt) lines **(Side Bar C)**. These regions are characterized by having a great deal of sunlight, minimal rain and high levels of evaporation.

Side Bar C Atmospheric circulation

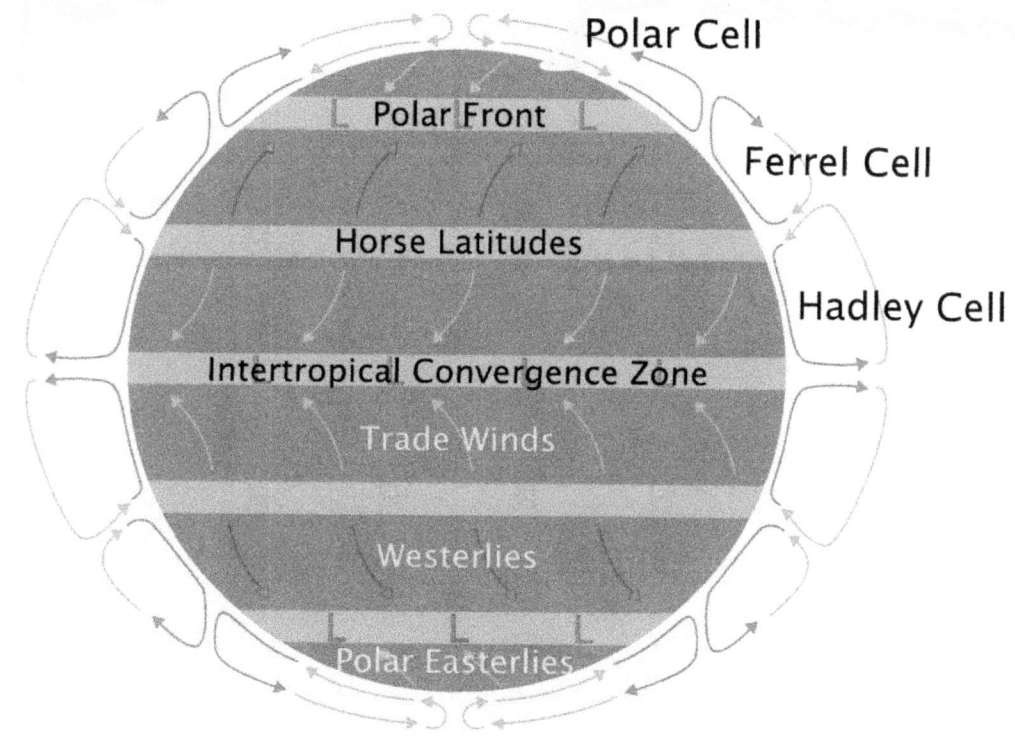

Although most deserts are within this latitudinal belt, there are some exceptions. There are deserts found in other regions of the world that are created by interactions with the land and geological setting. Some deserts are formed within **rain shadow zones**. As moist air passes over a mountain range, it ofeeten causes precipitation, leaving the air that moves down the other side of the mountain to be void of moisture. This creates a dry habitat, perfect for desert formation.

II. How Deserts Are Formed

The answer to the question "Why do deserts form?" seems obvious—sustained lack of rainfall—but the global and local climatic conditions that lead to such aridity are complex and an understanding of them helps explain such apparent anomalies as coastal deserts.

Deserts are among some of the most alien, inhospitable landscapes on the planet. Some of their most striking features—the vast fields of rubble, austerely patterned dunes, dry or seasonal riverbeds, gleaming rinks of sunbaked salt and the seeming near-absence of life might lead an observer to suspect they are the result of some great global catastrophe. In fact, just as any other **biome**, or major habitat, such as rain forest, tundra, and steppe, the world's deserts have evolved over millennia—the result of complex interactions between climate and geology.

Climate

The **desert climate,** in the Köppen climate classification *BWh* and *BWk* **(Side Bar D and E)** is a climate in which there is an excess of evaporation over precipitation. The typically bald, rocky, or sandy surfaces in desert climates hold little moisture and evaporate the little rainfall they receive. Covering 14.2 percent of the land area of the earth, hot deserts may be the most common type of climate on earth. Although no part of Earth is known for certain to be rainless, in the Atacama Desert in northern Chile, the average annual rainfall over a period of 17 years was only 0.20 inches. Some locations in the Sahara Desert, such as Kufra, Libya record only 0.034 inches of rainfall, annually. The official weather station in Death Valley, United States reports 2.4 inches but, in a 40-month period between 1931 and 1934, a total of 0.63 inches of rainfall was measured.

Side Bar D Hot and Cold Desert Regions

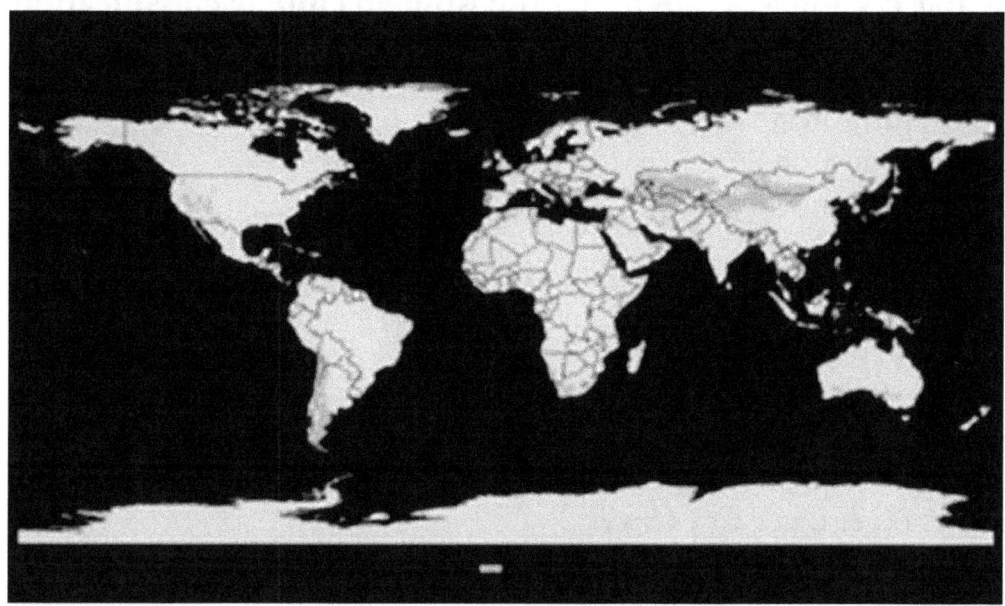

Regions with hot desert climates (*BWh*)

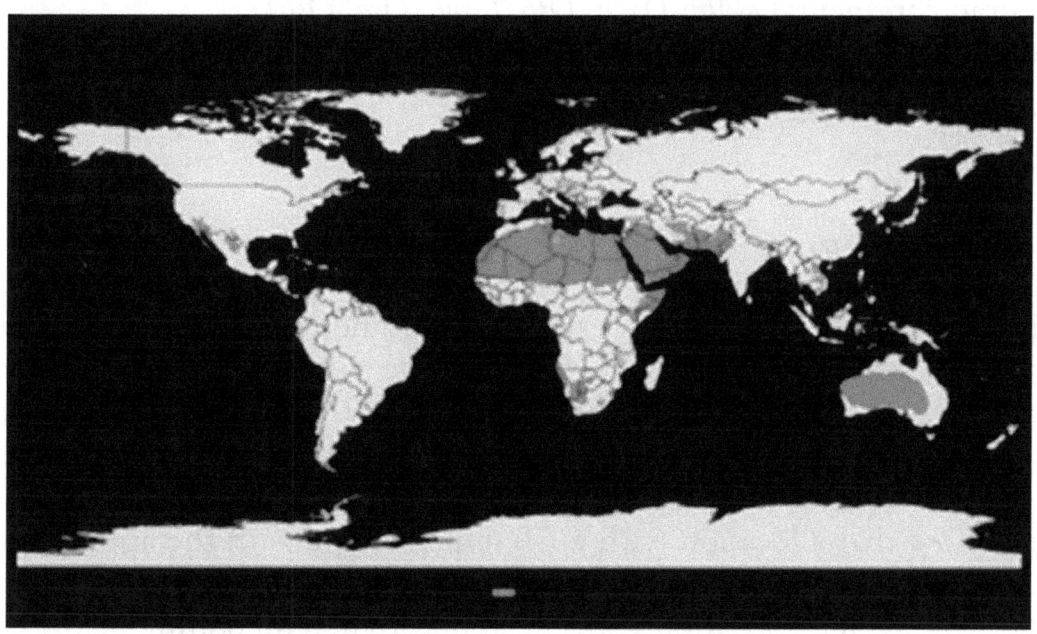

Regions with cold desert climates (*BWk*)

Side Bar E Climate types under the Köppen climate classification

Class A
Tropical rainforest *(Af)*
Tropical monsoon *(Am)*
Tropical savanna *(Aw, As)*

Class B
Desert (BWh, BWk)
Semi-arid (BSh, BSk)

Class C
Humid subtropical *(Cfa, Cwa)*
Oceanic *(Cfb, Cwb, Cfc, Cwc)*
Mediterranean *(Csa, Csb, Csc)*

Class D
Humid continental *(Dfa, Dwa, Dfb, Dwb, Dsa, Dsb)*
Subarctic *(Dfc, Dwc, Dfd, Dwd, Dsc, Dsd)*

Class E
Tundra *(ET)*
Ice cap *(EF)*
Alpine *(ET, EF)*

There are two variations of a desert climate: a hot desert climate (*BWh*), and a cold desert climate (*BWk*). To delineate "hot desert climates" from "cold desert climates", there are three widely used **isotherms**: most commonly a mean annual temperature of 64.4 degrees F, or sometimes a mean temperature of 32 degrees F or 26.6 degrees F in the coldest month, so that a location with a *BW* type climate with the appropriate temperature above whichever isotherm is being used is classified as "hot arid" (*BWh*), and a location with the appropriate temperature below the given isotherm is classified as "cold arid" (*BWk*).

Geography

Hot deserts (Figure 1) are lands of extremes: most of them are among the hottest, the driest and the sunniest places on Earth because of nearly constant high pressure; the nearly permanent removal of low pressure systems, dynamic fronts and atmospheric disturbances; sinking air motion; dry atmosphere near the surface and aloft; the exacerbated exposure to the sun where solar angles are always high.

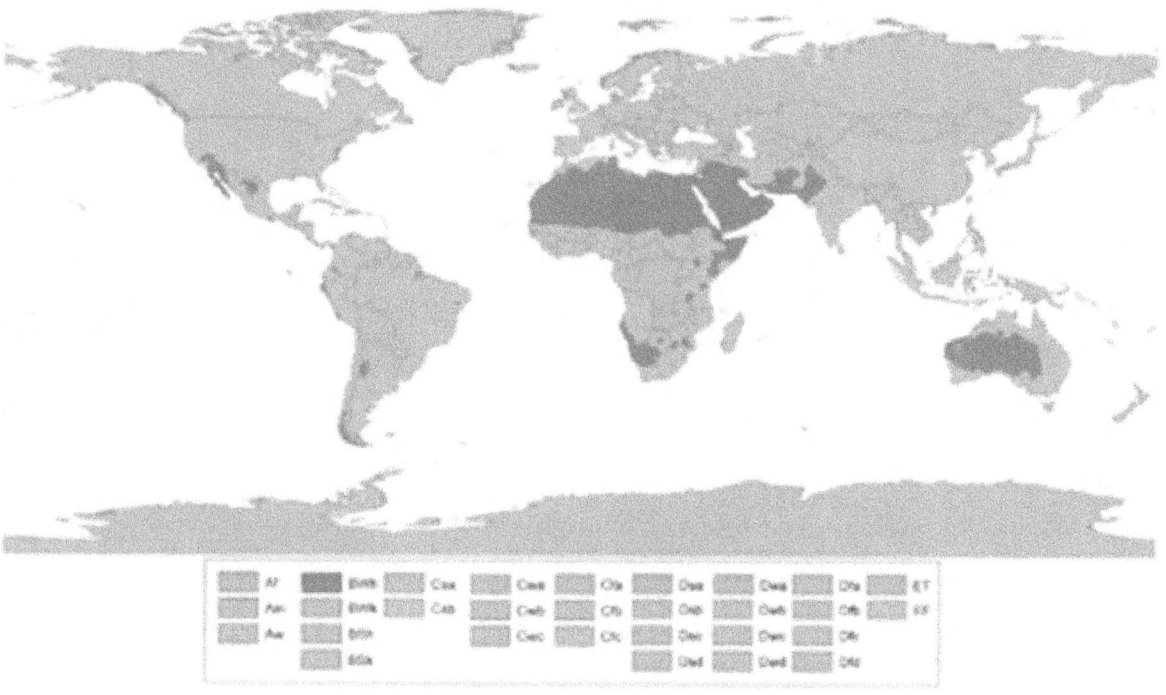

Fig. 1 Regions with hot desert climates

Hot deserts are lands of extremes: most of them are among the hottest, the driest and the sunniest places on Earth because of nearly constant high pressure; the nearly permanent removal of low pressure systems, dynamic fronts and atmospheric disturbances; sinking air motion; dry atmosphere near the surface and aloft; the exacerbated exposure to the sun where solar angles are always high.

Cold desert (Figure 2) climates are typically located in temperate zones, usually in the rain shadow of high mountains **(Side Bar F)**, which restrict precipitation from the westerly winds. An example of this is the Patagonian Desert in Argentina bounded by the Andes to its west. In the case of Central Asia, mountains restrict precipitation from the monsoon. The Kyzyl Kum, Taklamakan and Katpana Desert deserts of Central Asia and the drier portions of the Great Basin Desert of the western United States are other major examples of *BWk* climates. The Ladakh region, and the city of Leh in the Great Himalayas in India, also has a cold desert climate. This is also found in Europe, primarily in Bardenas Reales near Tudela, Navarre and high altitude parts of the Tabernas Desert in Almería, Spain.

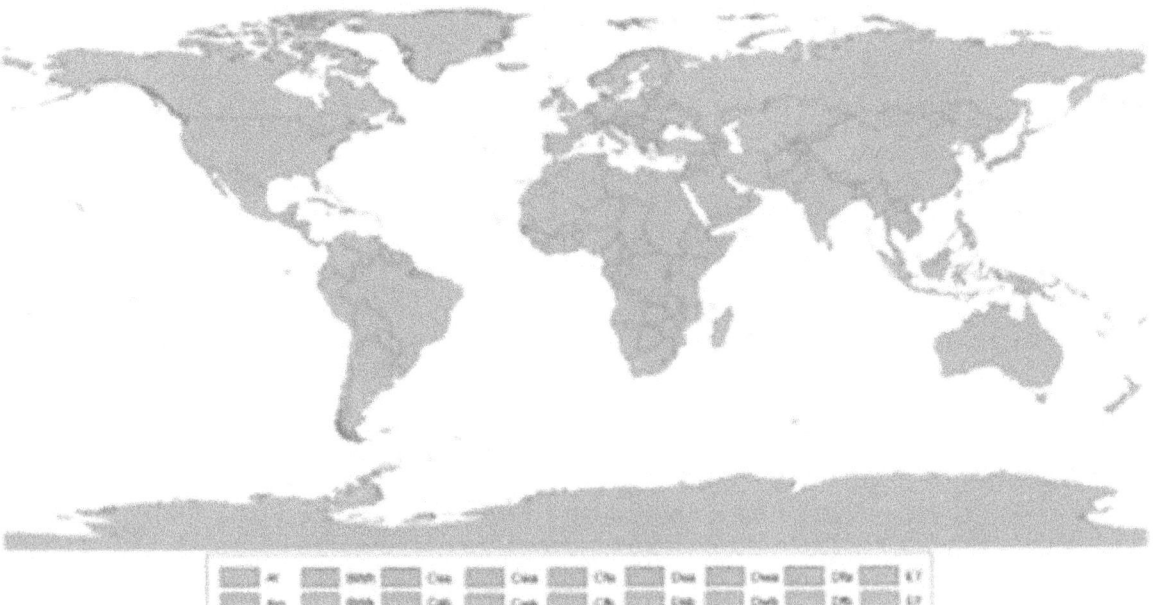

Fig. 2 Regions with cold desert climates

Side Bar F Rain Shadow

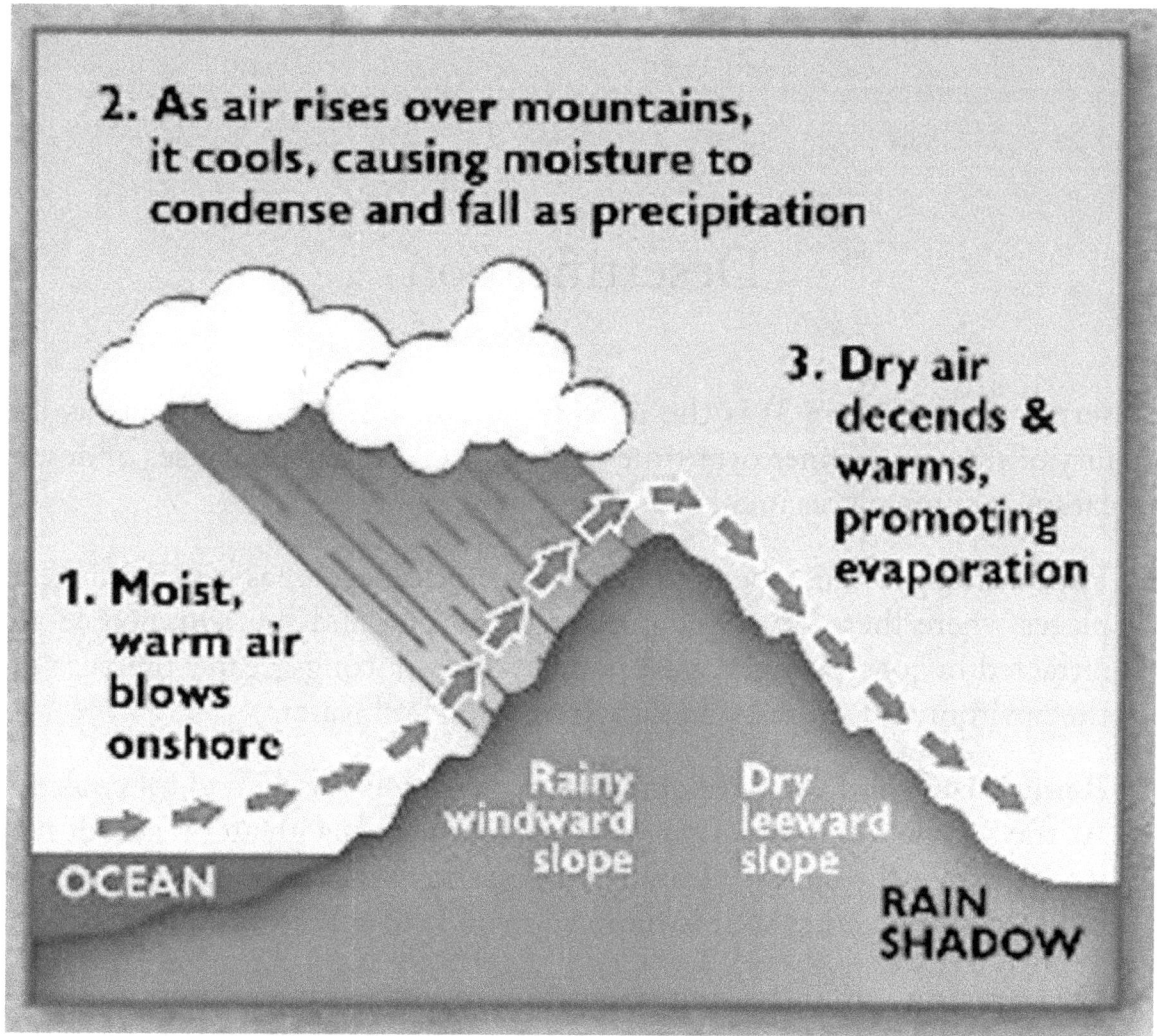

Arctic and Antarctic regions also receive very little precipitation during the year, owing to the exceptionally cold dry air; however, both of them are generally classified as having polar climates because they have average summer temperatures below 50 degrees F.

Desertification

Desertification **(Figure 3)** is the process of land turning into desert as the quality of the soil declines over time **(Side Bar G)**. The main causes of desertification in some places include:

- **Population growth** - the population in some desert areas is increasing. In places where there are developments in mining and tourism, people are attracted by jobs. An increased population is putting greater pressure on the environment for resources, such as wood and water.

- **Removal of wood** - in developing countries, people use wood for cooking. As the population in desert areas increases, there is a greater need for fuel wood. When the land is cleared of trees, the roots of the trees no longer hold the soil together so it is more vulnerable to soil erosion.

- **Overgrazing** - an increasing population results in larger desert areas being farmed. Sheep, cattle and goats are overgrazing the vegetation. This leaves the soil exposed to erosion.

- **Soil erosion** - this is made worse by overgrazing and the removal of wood. Population growth is the primary cause of soil erosion.

- **Climate change** - the global climate is getting warmer. In desert regions conditions are not only getting warmer but drier, too. On average there is less rain now in desert regions than there was 50 years ago.

Fig. 3 Desertification

Side Bar G Man-made Desert

How can desertification be reduced?

Desertification can be reduced in some places by adopting these strategies:

- **Planting more trees (Figure 4)** - the roots of trees hold the soil together and help to reduce soil erosion from wind and rain.

Fig. 4 Planting a tree

- **Improving the quality of the soil** - this can be managed by encouraging people to reduce the number of grazing animals they have and grow crops instead. The animal manure can be used to fertilize the crops grown.

Growing crops in this way can improve the quality of the soil as it is held together by the roots of plants and protected from erosion. This type of farming is more sustainable.

- **Water management** - water can be stored in earth dams in the wet season and used to irrigate crops during the dry season. This is an example of using appropriate technology to manage water supplies in the desert environment.

III. Major Deserts of the World

Deserts are found throughout the world, especially in Africa and Australia **(Side Bar H)**. The world's largest of the hot deserts is the Sahara **(Figure 5)**, which covers nearly all of northern Africa. The largest of the cold deserts of the world is Antarctica **(Figure 6)**, which covers the entire continent. As you can see, Antarctica is the only continent covered entirely by desert.

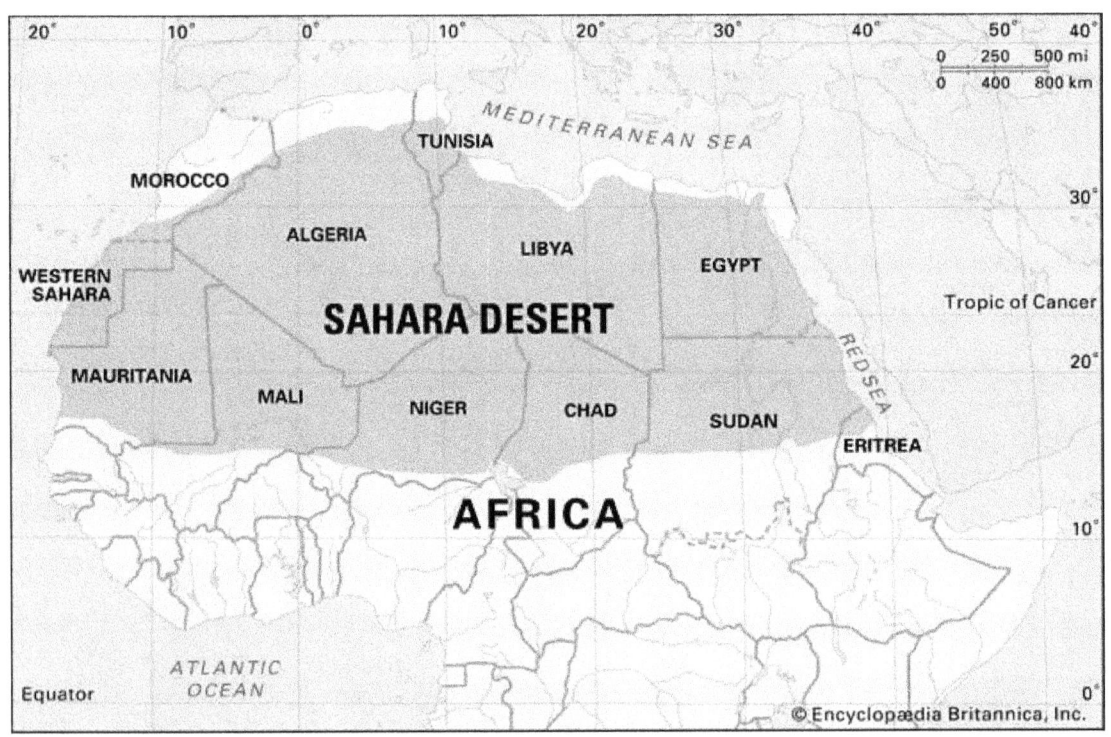

Fig. 5 Map of the Sahara Desert

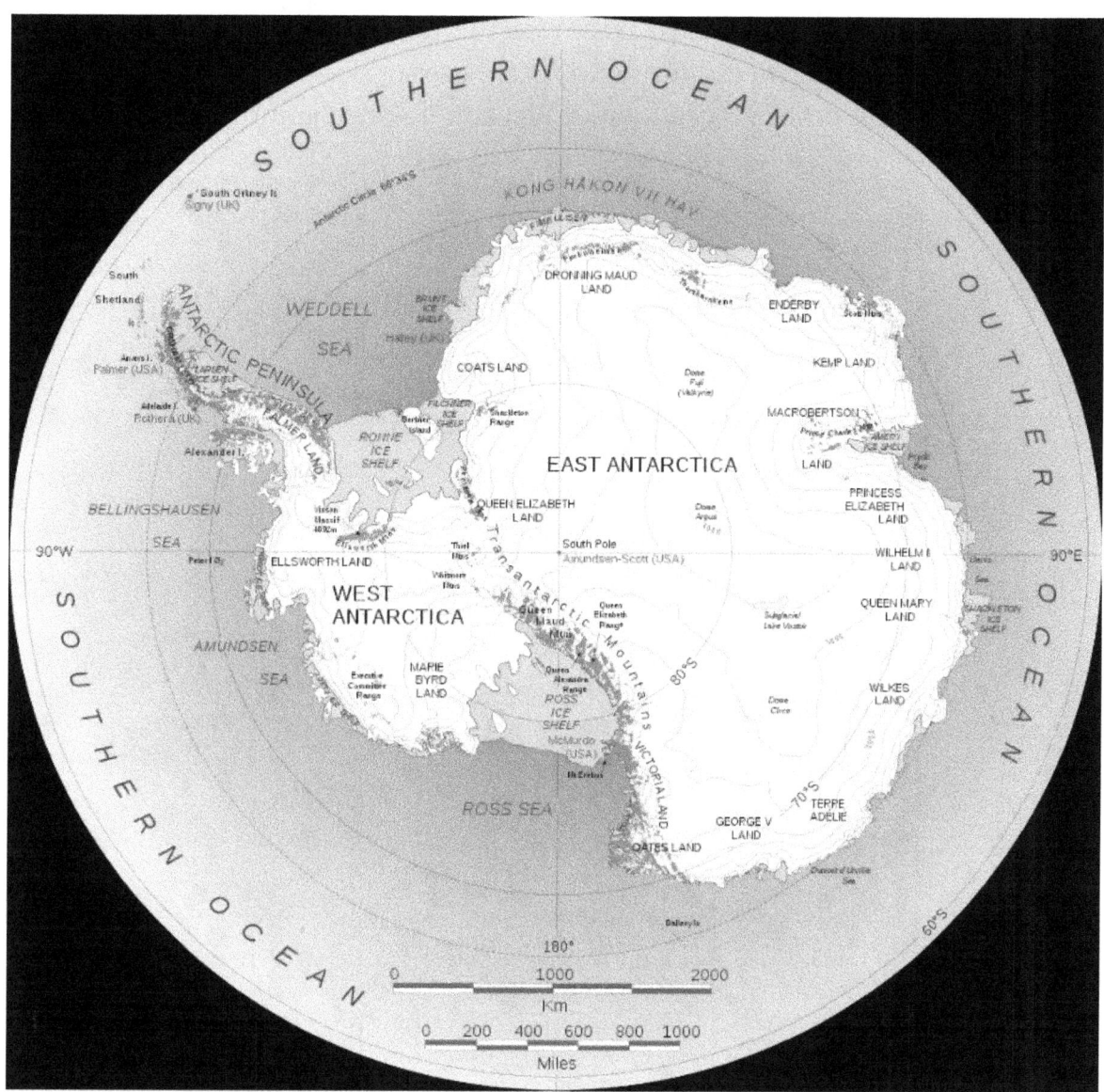

Fig. 6 Map of Antarctica

- Sand covers only about 20 percent of the deserts of the Earth. Most of the sand is in sand sheets and sand seas—vast regions of undulating dunes **(Figure 7)** resembling ocean waves "frozen" in an instant of time.

Fig. 7 Undulating Dune

- Nearly 50 percent of desert surfaces are plains where **eolian deflation**—removal of fine-grained material by the wind **(Side Bar I)**—has exposed loose gravels consisting predominantly of pebbles but with occasional cobbles.

- The remaining surfaces of arid lands are composed of exposed bedrock outcrops, desert soils, and **fluvial deposits** including alluvial fans, playas, desert lakes, and oases. Bedrock outcrops commonly occur as small mountains surrounded by extensive erosional plains.

- Oases are vegetated areas moistened by springs, wells, or by irrigation. Many are artificial. Oases are often the only places in deserts that support crops and permanent habitation.

- Now, let's look at some of the largest deserts throughout the world.

Side Bar H World Deserts

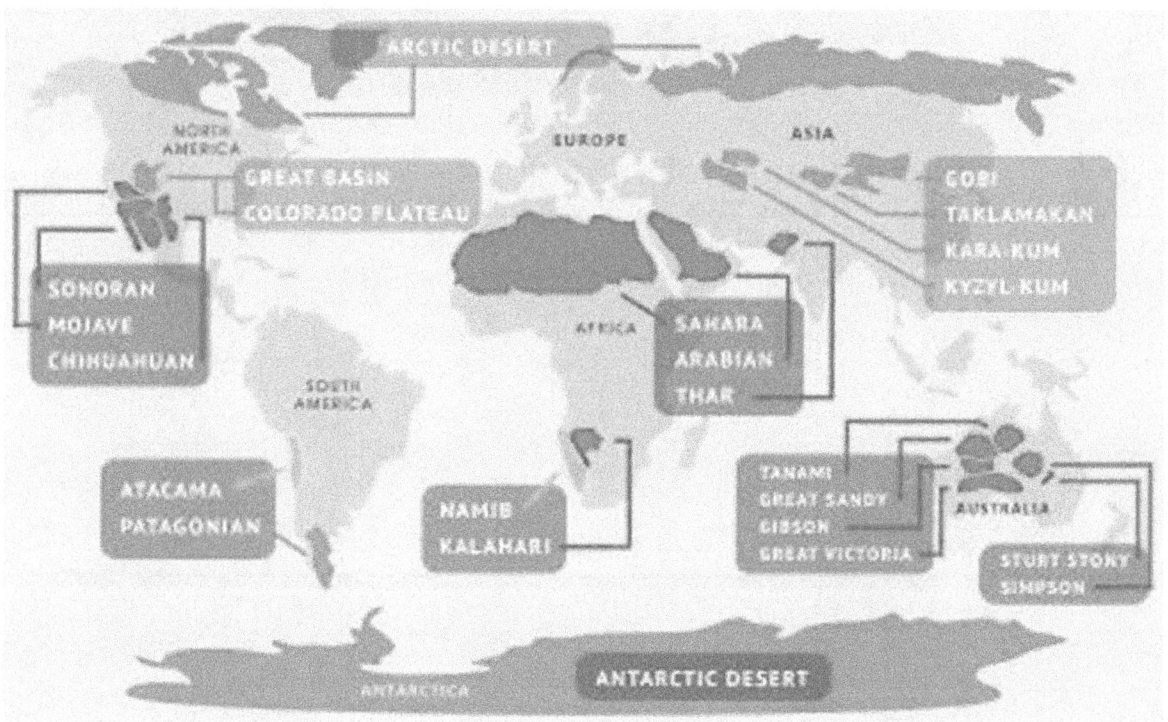

Side Bar I Movement of Sand Dune

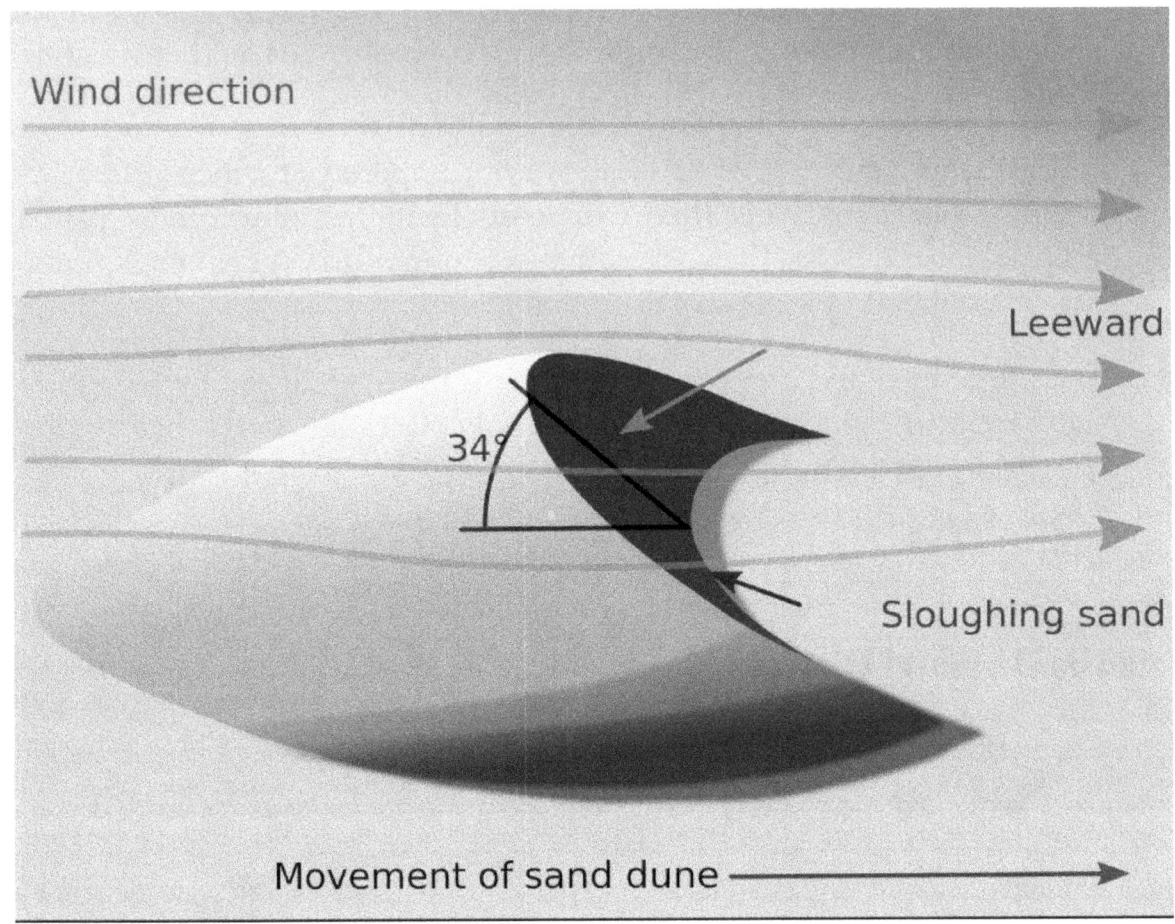

Deserts of Antarctica

The two largest deserts on Earth are in the polar areas. The Antarctic Polar Desert **(Figure 8)** covers the continent of Antarctica and has a size of about 5.5 million square miles. The second-largest desert is the Arctic Polar Desert **(Side Bar J)**. It extends over parts of Alaska, Canada, Greenland, Iceland, Norway, Sweden, Finland, and Russia. It has a surface area of about 5.4 million square miles.

Fig. 8 Polar Desert – Antarctica

Side Bar J Arctic Desert

Polar deserts are areas with annual precipitation less than 9 inches and a mean temperature during the warmest month of less than 50 degrees F. Polar deserts on the Earth cover nearly 1,930,511 square miles and are mostly bedrock or gravel plains. Sand dunes are not prominent features in these deserts, but snow dunes occur commonly in areas where precipitation is locally more abundant. Temperature changes in polar deserts frequently cross the freezing point of water.

Deserts of Africa

The Sahara

The Sahara **(Figure 9)** is the largest hot desert in the world, and the third largest desert behind Antarctica and the Arctic, which are both cold deserts. The Sahara is one of the harshest environments on Earth, covering 3.6 million square miles, nearly a third of the African continent, about the size of the United States (including Alaska and Hawaii). The name of the desert comes from the Arabic word ṣaḥrā', which means "desert".

Fig, 9 Sand dunes in the Sahara, Morocco

The Sahara is bordered by the Atlantic Ocean on the west, the Red Sea on the east, the Mediterranean Sea on the north and the Sahel Savannah on the south. The enormous desert spans 11 countries: Algeria, Chad, Egypt, Libya, Mali, Mauritania, Morocco, Niger, Western Sahara, Sudan and Tunisia.

The Sahara desert has a variety of land features but is most famous for the sand dune fields often depicted in movies. The dunes can reach almost 600 feet high but they cover only about 15 percent of the entire desert. Other topographical features include mountains, plateaus, sand- and gravel-covered plains, salt flats, basins and depressions. Mount Koussi, an extinct volcano in Chad, is the highest point in the Sahara at 11,204 feet, and the Qattara Depression in Egypt is the deepest point of the Sahara, at 436 feet below sea level.

Although water is scarce across the entire region, the Sahara contains two permanent rivers, the Nile and the Niger, at least twenty seasonal lakes and huge **aquifers**, which are the primary sources of water in the more than 90 major desert oases. Water management authorities once feared the aquifers in the Sahara would soon dry up because of overuse; but a study published in the journal Geophysical Research Letters in 2013, details the discovery of the 'fossil', nonrenewable aquifers, which were still being fed via rain and runoff. Ergs **(Figure 10)** or sand sheets and dunes cover approximately 25 percent of the surface of the Sahara An **erg** (also sand sea or dune sea, or sand sheet if it lacks dunes) is a broad, flat area of desert covered with wind-swept sand with little or no vegetative cover, Strictly speaking, an erg is defined as a desert area that contains more than 48 sq miles of aeolian or wind-blown sand and where sand covers more than 20 percent of the surface.

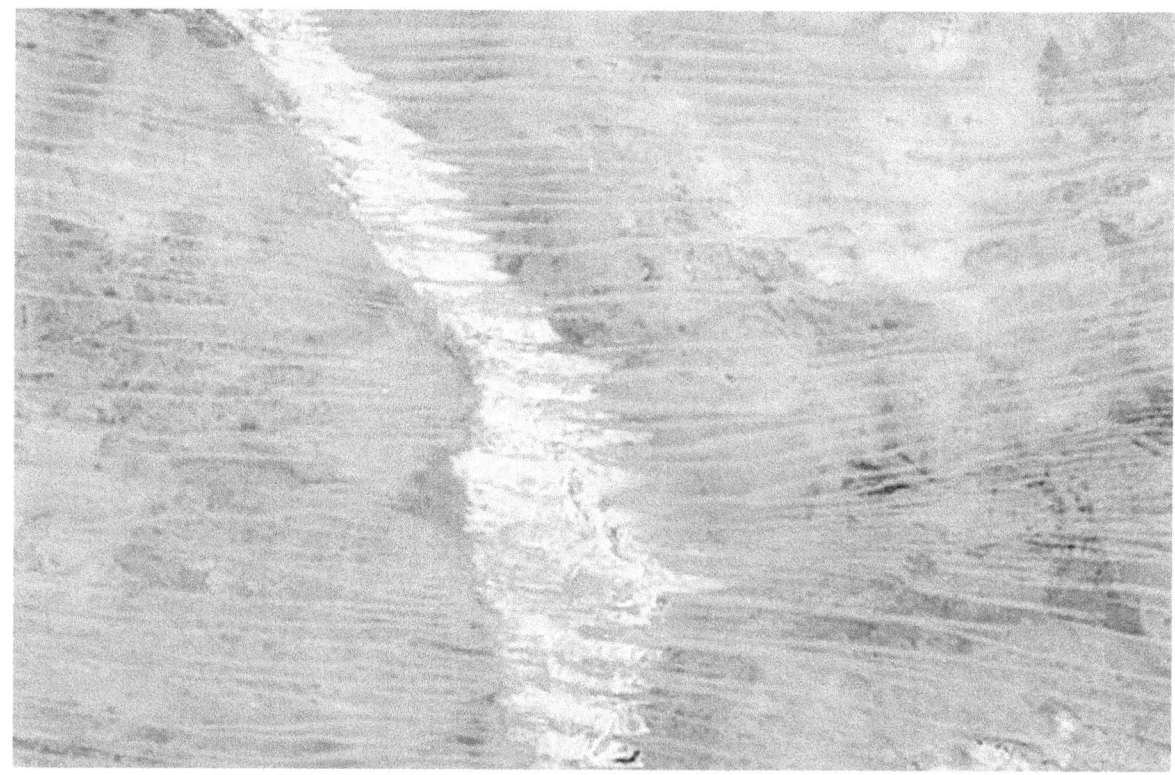

Fig, 10 Ergs or seas of sand

By nature, ergs are very active. Smaller dunes form and migrate along the flanks of the larger dunes and sand ridges. Occasional precipitation fills basins formed by the dunes; as the water evaporates, salt deposits are lefeet behind.

Individual dunes in ergs typically have widths, lengths, or both dimensions greater than 1,600 feet. Both the regional extent of their sand cover and the complexity and great size of their dunes distinguish ergs from dune fields. The depth of sand in ergs varies widely around the world, ranging from only a few inches deep in the Selima Sand Sheet of Southern Egypt, to approximately 3.3 feet) in the Simpson Desert, and 69–141 feet in the Sahara. This is far shallower than ergs in prehistoric times where evidence in the geological record indicates some Mesozoic and Paleozoic ergs reached a mean depth of several hundred feet.

The principal types of dunes include tied dunes, which form in the lee of hills or other obstacles; parabolic blowout dunes; crescent-shaped **barchans and transverse dunes (Figure 11); longitudinal seifs (Figure 12)**; and the massive, complex forms associated with sand seas. Several pyramidal dunes in the Sahara attain heights of nearly 500 feet, while *draa*, the mountainous sand ridges that dominate the ergs, are said to reach 1,000 feet. An unusual phenomenon associated with desert sands is their "singing" or booming. Various hypotheses have been advanced to explain the phenomenon, such as those based on the piezoelectric property of crystalline quartz, but the mystery remains unsolved.

Fig. 11 Barchans and transverse dune

Fig. 12 View looking upward to top of a longitudinal dune

The Arabian Desert (Figure 13)

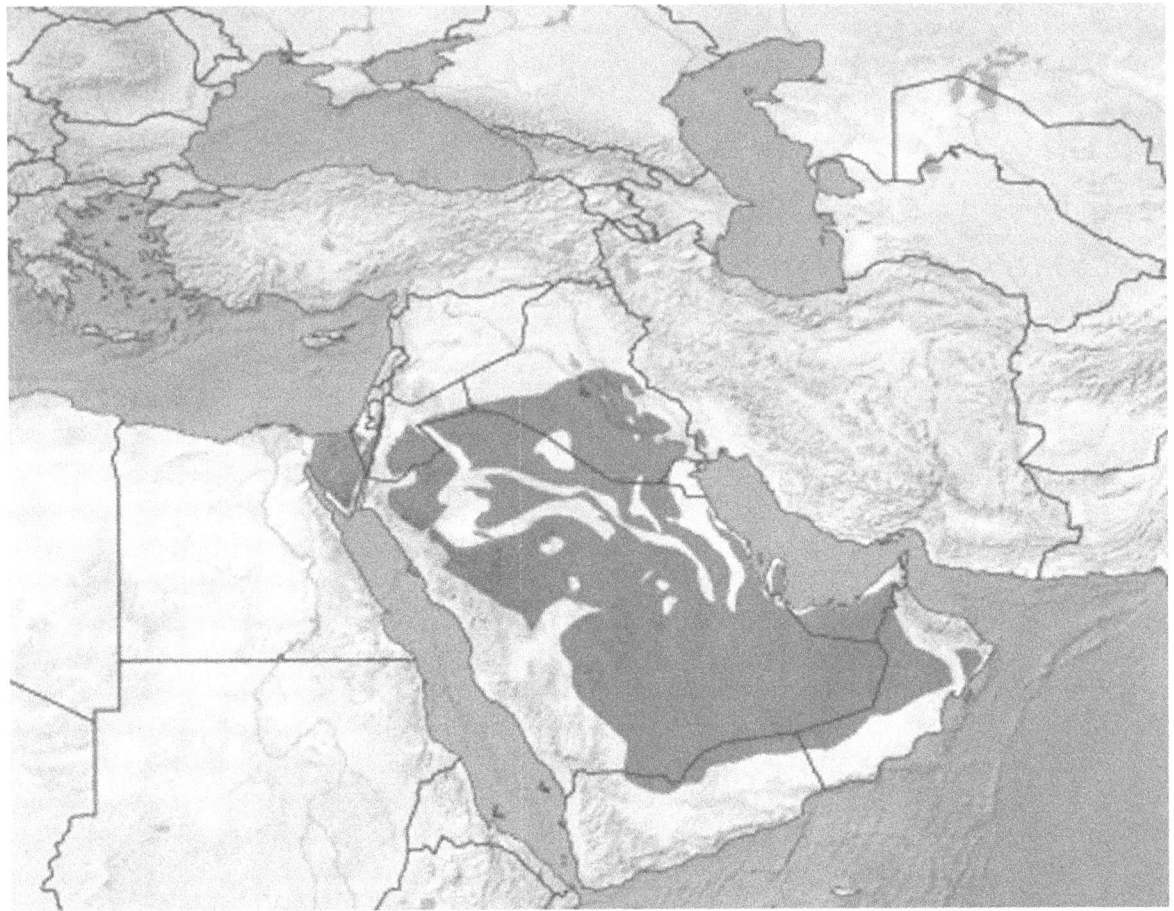

Fig. 13 Map of the Arabian Desert

The Arabian Desert (**Figure 14**) is bordered to the north by the Syrian Desert, to the northeast and east by the Persian Gulf and the Gulf of Oman, to the southeast and south by the Arabian Sea and the Gulf of Aden, and to the west by the Red Sea. A large part of the Arabian Desert lies within the modern kingdom of Saudi Arabia. Yemen, on the coast of the Gulf of Aden and the Red Sea, borders the desert to the southwest. Oman, bulging out into the Gulf of Oman, lies at the eastern edge of the desert. The sheikhdoms of the United Arab Emirates and Qatar to the west stretch along the southern coast of the Persian Gulf at the desert's northeastern limit. The emirate of

Kuwait abuts the northern Persian Gulf between Saudi Arabia and Iraq. In the northwest the desert extends into Jordan.

Fig. 14 The Arabian Desert

Seen from the air, the Arabian Desert appears as a vast expanse of light sand-colored terrain with an occasional indistinct line of escarpments or mountain ranges, black lava flows, or reddish systems of desert dunes stretching to the horizon. Camel trails crisscross the surface between watering places. On the ground, features become distinctly individual and the relief seems more prominent. Vegetation at first seems nonexistent, but the discerning eye can find sparse patches of growth on the surface, or bits of green where shrubs strive to survive. There is almost always a breeze, which changes seasonally to winds of gale force. Cold or hot, those air currents chill the body or roast it. The Sun and Moon are bright in clear skies, although dust and humidity may lower visibility.

The Arabian Desert spreads across 22° of latitude, from 12° to 34° north; although much of the desert lies north of the Tropic of Cancer, it usually is considered a tropical desert. Summer heat is intense, reaching temperatures as high as 130o F in places. In the interior, the heat is dry. Coastal regions and some highlands, however, are subject to high summer humidity, with dew and fog at night or early morning. Rainfall throughout the desert averages less than 4 inches a year but can range from 0 to 20 inches. Interior skies are usually clear except for intermittent winter rains, spring hazes, or dust storms. Torrential rains flood the main drainage basins infrequently. Winters are invigoratingly cool, with the coldest weather occurring at high elevations and in the far north. A minimum temperature recorded at Ṭurayf on Tapline (the Trans-Arabian Pipeline) in 1950 was 10 degrees F and was accompanied by a major snowfall and about 1 inch of ice on ponds. Occasional summer rains in the Rubʿ al-Khali accompany the monsoon winds from the Indian Ocean. Winter rains may occur in the northern Rubʿ al-Khali. The most arid part of the Arabian Desert appears to be on the western margin of the Rubʿ al-Khali, north of Wadi Al-Dawāsir.

The Arabian Desert, a vast desert wilderness stretching from Yemen to the Persian Gulf and from Oman to Jordan and Iraq, is the largest desert in Asia at 900,000 square miles and occupies most of the Arabian Peninsula. Actually, this desert is located in the Middle East and is often considered Africa, though it is in extreme western Asia.

Gazelles, oryx, sand cats, and spiny-tailed lizards are just some of the desert-adapted species that survive in this extreme environment, which features everything from red dunes to deadly quicksand. The climate is mostly dry and temperatures oscillate between very high heat and seasonal night time freezes. It is part of the deserts and xeric shrub lands biome and the Palearctic realm.

The Arabian Desert has a subtropical, hot desert climate, similar to the climate of the Sahara Desert; the world's largest hot desert. The Arabian Desert is actually an extension of the Sahara Desert over the Arabian Peninsula. The sunshine duration in the Arabian Desert is very high by global standards, between 2,900 hours (66.2 percent of daylight hours) and 3,600 hours (82.1 percent of daylight hours), but it is typically around 3,400 hours (77.6 percent of daylight hours), thus clear-sky conditions prevail over the region and cloudy periods are intermittent. Even though the sun and moon are bright, dust and humidity cause lower visibility at ground level. The temperatures remain high all year round. Average high temperatures in summer are generally over 104 degrees F at low elevations, and can even soar to 118 degrees F at extremely low elevations, especially along the Persian Gulf near sea level. Average low temperatures in summer remain high, over 68 degrees F and sometimes over 86 degrees F in the southernmost regions. Record high temperatures are above 122 degrees F in much of the desert, as a result of the very low elevation.

Riyadh, the capital of Saudi Arabia, lies in the center of the desert with more than 7 million inhabitants. Other large cities, such as Dubai, Abu Dhabi, or Kuwait City, lie on the coast of the Persian Gulf.

The Syrian Desert

Syrian Desert **(Figure 15)** is an arid wasteland of southwestern Asia, extending northward from the Arabian Peninsula over much of northern Saudi Arabia, eastern Jordan, southern Syria, and western Iraq **(Side Bar K)**. Also known as the Syrian steppe, the Jordanian steppe, or the Badia, is a region of desert, semi-desert and steppe covering 200,000 square miles of the Middle East, including parts of south-eastern Syria, northeastern Jordan, northern Saudi Arabia, and western Iraq. It accounts for 85 percent of the land area of Jordan and 55 percent of Syria. To the south it borders and merges into the Arabian Desert. The land is open, rocky or gravelly desert pavement, cut with occasional wadis. Receiving on the average less than 5 inches of rainfall annually and largely covered by lava flows, it formed a nearly impenetrable barrier between the populated areas of the Levant and Mesopotamia until modern times.

Fig. 15 The Syrian Desert

Side Bar K The Syrian Desert

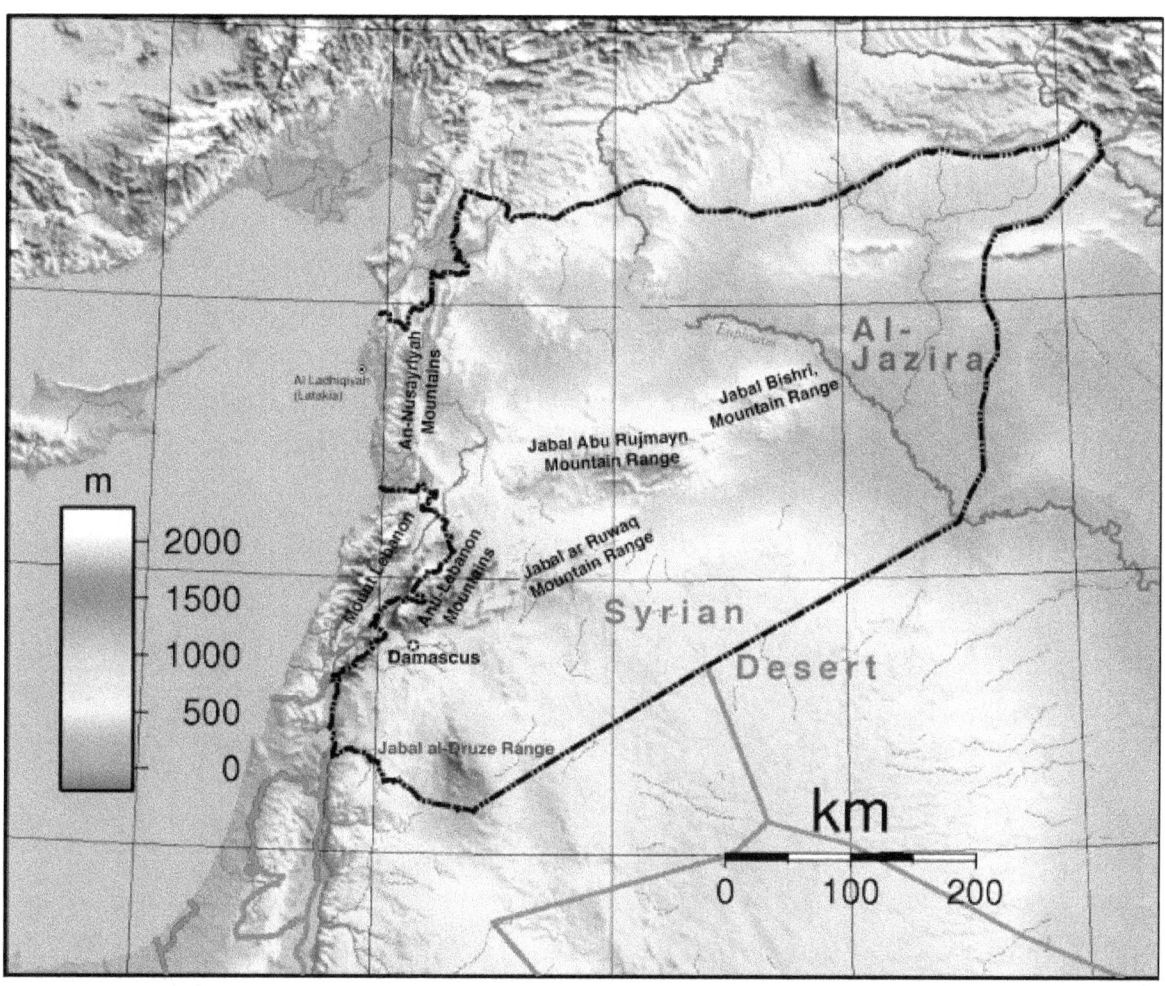

The Syrian Desert extends northward from the Arabian Peninsula over much of northern Saudi Arabia, eastern Jordan, southern Syria, and western Iraq. It is sometimes considered extreme western Asia or extreme eastern Africa, if Arabia is considered part of Africa because of the narrow land strip.

The Kalahari Desert (Side Bar L)

A geological wonder, the Kalahari Desert (**Figure 16**) is part of the huge sand basin that reaches from the Orange River up to Angola, in the west to Namibia and in the east to Zimbabwe. The sand masses of wind-shaped sand that are so common in the Kalahari landscape were created by the erosion of soft stone formations. Thanks to vegetation in the area, the dunes were stabilized 10,000 to 20,000 years ago. Strangely enough, the grasses, thorny shrubs and Acacia trees can survive long drought periods of more than 10 months a year. Some scientists don't consider the Kalahari a true desert because some parts of the Kalahari receive more than 10 inches of rain in a year. Animals that live in the region include brown hyena, lion, meerkat, several species of antelope, and many types of birds and reptiles.

Fig. 16 The Kalahari Desert

The Kalahari Desert ranges over more than 347, 492 square miles in the depths of Southern Africa. In total, it crosses the borders of three countries. In the north-east, it dominates portions of Botswana. There, it's a safari-goer's mecca; a place to glimpse stalking leopards, zooming cheetahs, and huge

Side Bar L 10 Interesting Kalahari Desert Facts

1. Is the Kalahari Desert hot or cold?

The temperatures in the Kalahari Desert are extreme, with summers being very hot while winter temperatures can go below 32 degrees F at night. This is a result of the Kalahari's relatively high altitude and predominantly clear, dry air.

2. What is the temperature range in the Kalahari Desert?

In summer, temperatures can reach 115 degrees F; on winter nights, lows can drop to 7 degrees F.

3. How large is the Kalahari Desert?

The Kalahari Desert covers approximately 350,000 square miles. It is a gently undulating, sand-covered plain, and all of it is 2953 feet or more above sea level.

4. Why is the Kalahari a desert?

One of the most surprising Kalahari Desert facts is that it is not a desert in the strictest sense of the word. It is a semi-desert. The driest areas receive 4 to 8 inches of rain per year and the wettest can receive more than 20 inches in very wet years.

Traditionally, an area is classified a desert if it receives less than 10 inches of rain annually. A more accurate definition of a desert is a region in which "the evaporation rate is twice as great as the precipitation". This is true for the southwestern half of the Kalahari. The northeastern portion, however, receives much more rainfall and, climatically, cannot qualify as a desert; and yet, it is totally lacking in surface water. This is because rain drains instantly through the deep sands here, leaving the substrate completely devoid of moisture.

5. What countries make up the Kalahari Desert?

The Kalahari Desert covers much of Botswana, the eastern third of Namibia and the northernmost part of the Northern Cape Province in South Africa.

6. What wildlife can be found in the Kalahari Desert?

The wildlife found in the Kalahari Desert has to be able to survive the arid conditions. The wetter north has a richer and greater variety of wildlife than the dryer south.

Arid-adapted game includes springbok, gemsbok (oryx), wildebeest, kudu, steenbok and duiker. The Kalahari is home to desert specialties such as meerkat, bat-eared foxes, cape fox and brown hyena. One of the more unexpected Kalahari Desert facts is that all three African big cats can be found here —cheetah, leopard and the famous black-maned Kalahari lions.

Birdlife includes the secretary bird, Kori bustard, ostrich and a variety of birds of prey, including the martial eagle, giant eagle owl, falcons, goshawks, kestrels and kites. The landscape is dotted with huge nests of sociable weavers, built precariously on trees and telegraph poles.

Many reptiles also live in the Kalahari, including Cape cobras, puff adders, and numerous lizard species. Remarkably some amphibians are also able to survive here, including the bushveld rain frog and the tremolo sand frog. It is incredible to hear the frog chorus commence as soon as the rains arrive.

7. What kinds of plants are in the Kalahari Desert?

The dryer south-western Kalahari Desert has few trees or large bushes—just scattered drought-tolerant shrubs and grass tussocks. Hoodia cactus grow here, used for thousands of years by the San people to ease hunger and thirst. Other edible plants found here include tsamma melons and gemsbok cucumbers – used by both animals and humans.

The central Kalahari, with more rain, has scattered trees (several species of Acacia) and more shrubs and grasses. In the wetter north and east, there are woodlands mainly made up of camelthorn acacias. Endemic to the Kalahari, the camelthorn is a crucial part of the desert ecosystem, producing nutrients that encourage other plants to grow around its base and providing shade for animals. Other trees that grow in this area include shepherd's tree, blackthorn and silver cluster-leaf.

8. What type of desert is the Kalahari?

The Kalahari Desert is a large semi-arid sandy savannah. Even where the Kalahari "desert" is dry enough to qualify as a desert in the sense of having low precipitation; it is not strictly speaking a desert because the ground cover is too dense.

9. How is the Kalahari related to African deserts?

The Kalahari is the southernmost desert in Africa. It is the sixth biggest desert by area on Earth and the second biggest in Africa after the Sahara. In the southwest it merges with the Namib, the coastal desert of Namibia.

10. Where is the Kalahari Desert located on a map?

The Kalahari Desert is located in Southern Africa, covering much of Botswana, the eastern third of Namibia and the northernmost part of South Africa's Northern Cape Province.

Deserts of the Americas

The North American Deserts

North America has four major deserts **(Figure 17)**: Great Basin, Mohave, Chihuahuan and Sonoran. All but the Sonoran Desert have cold winters. Freezing temperatures are even more limiting to plant life than is aridity, so colder deserts are poorer in both species and life forms, especially succulents.

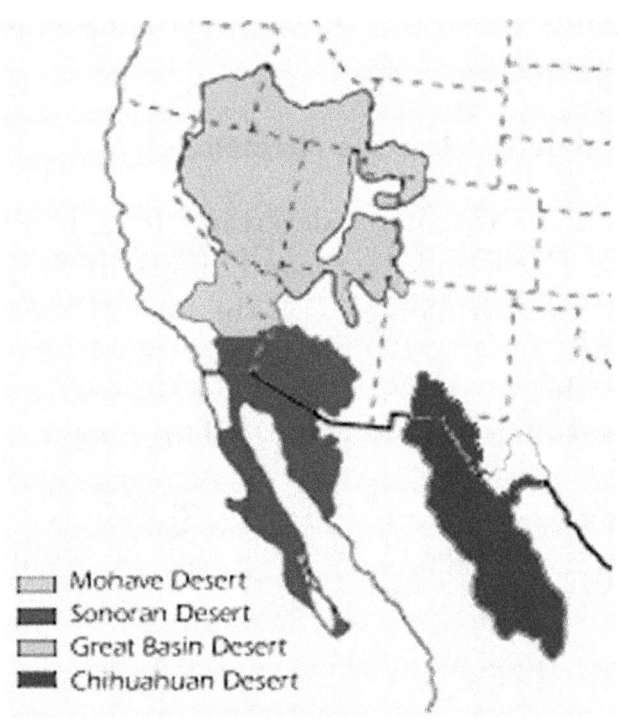

Fig. 17 The four North American deserts

The Great Basin Desert

The Great Basin Desert **(Figure 18)** is both the highest-elevation and northernmost of the four and has very cold winters. The seasonal distribution of precipitation varies with latitude, but temperatures limit the growing season to the summer. Vegetation is dominated by a few species of low, small-leafed shrubs; there are almost no trees or succulents and not many annuals. The indicator plant, the most common or conspicuous one used to identify an area, is big sagebrush (*Artemisia tridentata*), which often grows in nearly pure stands over huge vistas, such cold shrub/deserts in the "Old World" are called steppes.

Fig. 18 The Great Basin Desert

The Mojave Desert (*moh-HAH-vee*) (Side Bar M)

The Mojave Desert **(Figure 19)** is characterized largely by its winter rainy season. Hard freezes are common but not as severe as in the Great Basin Desert. The perennial vegetation is composed mostly of low shrubs; annuals carpet the ground in wet years. There are many species of these two life forms, but few succulents and trees grow there. The only common tree species is the characteristic Joshua tree (*Yucca brevifolia*) **(Side Bar N)**, an **arborescent** yucca that forms extensive woodlands above 3000 feet elevation.

Side Bar M Desert Pavement of the Mojave

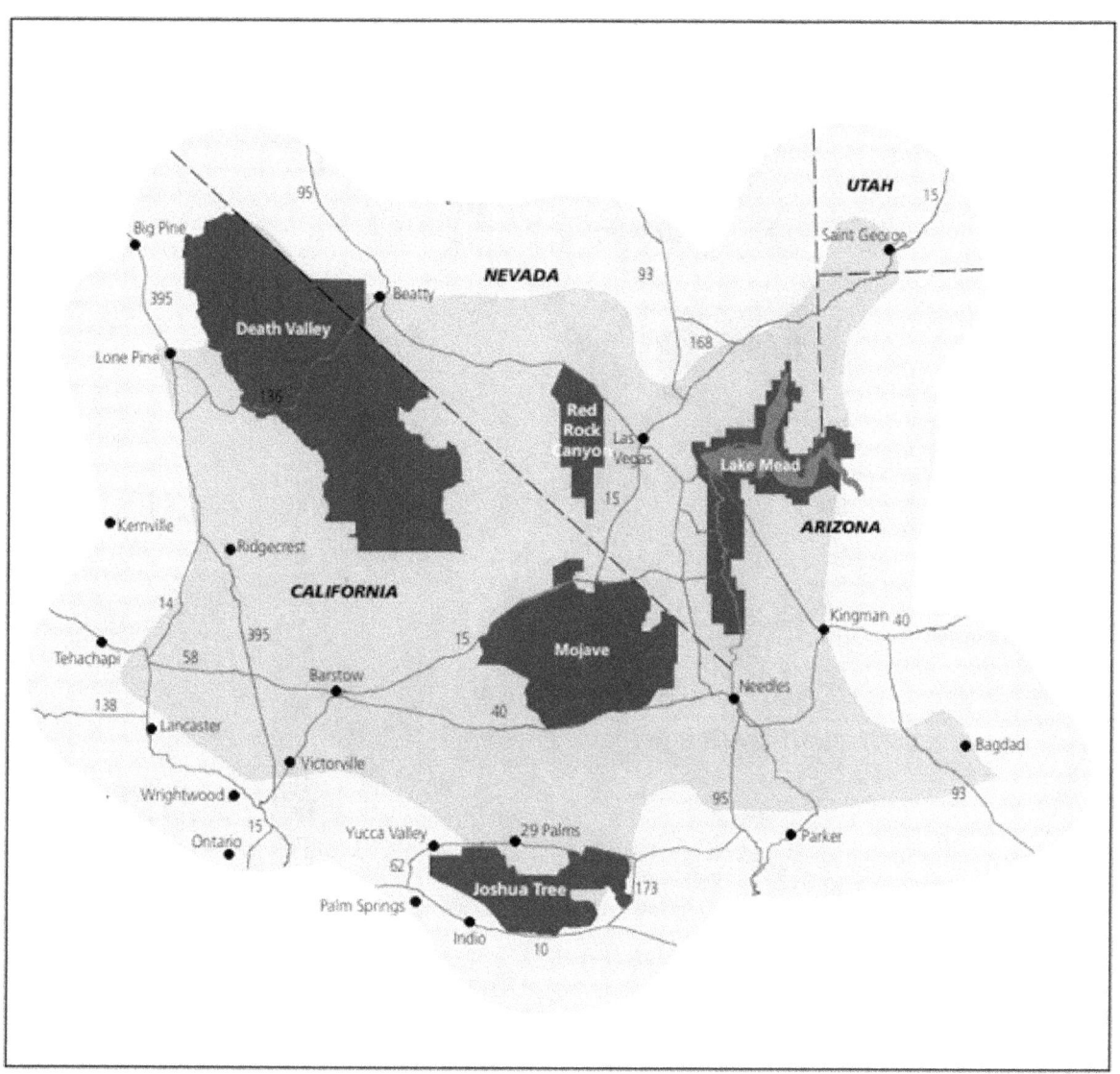

Fig. 19 Map of the Mohave Desert

Side Bar N The Joshua tree

The Chihuahuan Desert

Though the Chihuahuan Desert **(Figure 20)** is the southernmost, it lies at a fairly high elevation and is not protected by any barrier from arctic air masses, so hard winter freezes are common. Its vegetation consists of many species of low shrubs, leaf succulents, and small cacti **(Side Bar O)**. Trees are rare. Rainfall is predominantly in the summer, but in the northern end there is occasionally enough winter rain to support massive blooms of spring annuals. The Chihuahuan Desert is unexpectedly rich in species despite the winter cold.

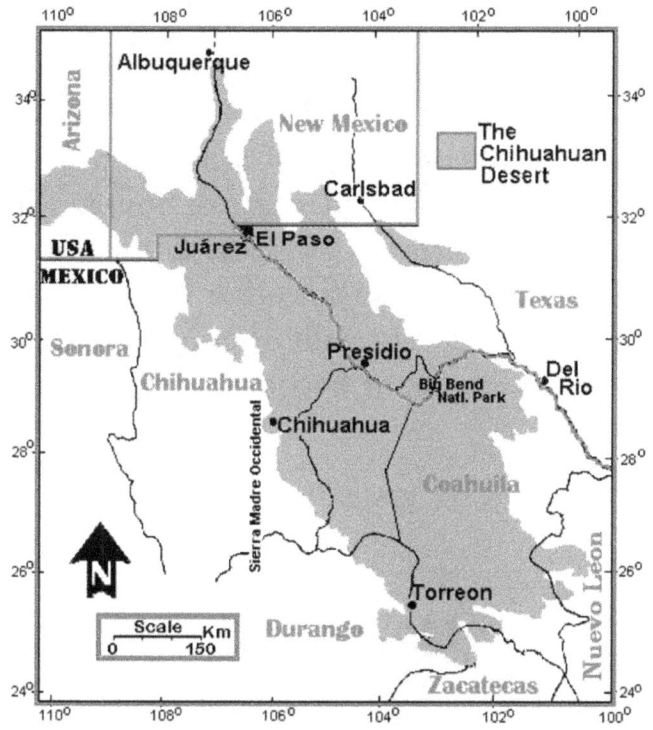

Fig. 20 Map of the Chihuahuan Desert

Side Bar O the Chihuahuan Desert

The Sonoran Desert

The Sonoran Desert **(Figure 21)** as currently defined covers approximately 100,000 square miles and includes most of the southern half of Arizona, southeastern California, most of the Baja California peninsula, the islands of the Gulf of California, and much of the state of Sonora, Mexico. It is lush in comparison to most other deserts. Two visually dominant life forms of plants distinguish the Sonoran Desert from the other North American deserts: legume trees and columnar cacti, especially the saguaro cactus **(Figure 22)**. It also supports many other life forms encompassing a rich spectrum of some 2,000 species of plants.

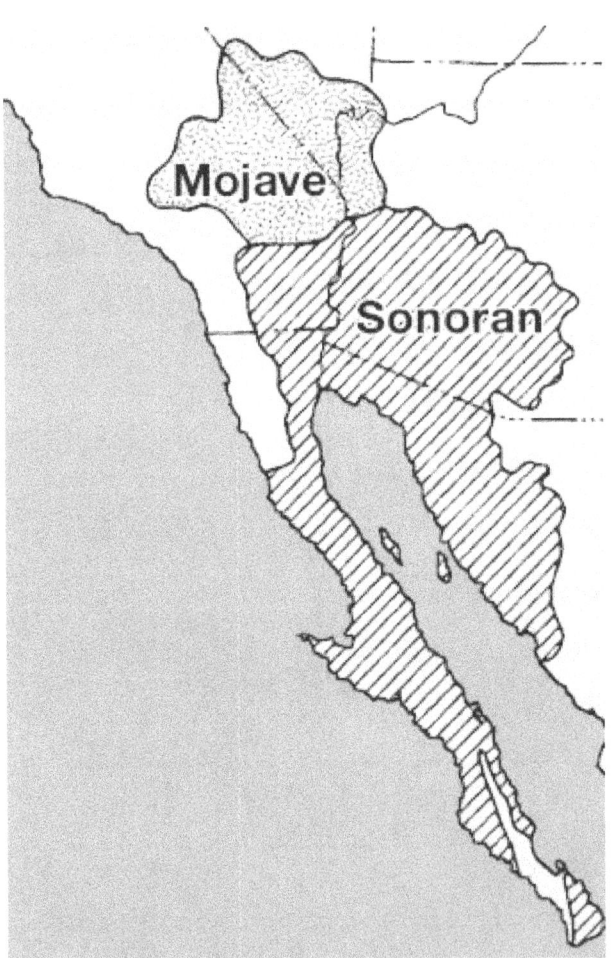

Fig. 21 Map of the Sonoran Desert

Fig. 22 The Sonoran Desert Landscape

The amount and seasonality of rainfall are defining characteristics of the Sonoran Desert. Much of the area has a bi-seasonal rainfall pattern, though even during the rainy seasons most days are sunny. From December to March frontal storms from North Pacific Ocean occasionally bring widespread, gentle rain to the northwestern areas. From July to mid-September, the summer monsoon brings surges of wet tropical air and frequent but localized violent thunderstorms.

The Sonoran Desert prominently differs from the other three North American Deserts in having mild winters; most of the area rarely experiences frost. About half of the biota is tropical in origin, with life cycles attuned to the brief summer rainy season. The winter rains, when ample, produce huge populations of annuals, which comprise half of the species in the flora.

Subdivisions of the Sonoran Desert

Forrest Shreve defined seven vegetative subdivisions **(Figure 23)** in the 1950s. One, the Foothills of Sonora, has since been reclassified as foothills thornscrub, a non-desert biome. The status of two other subdivisions - Arizona Upland and Plains of Sonora - may also be reclassified.

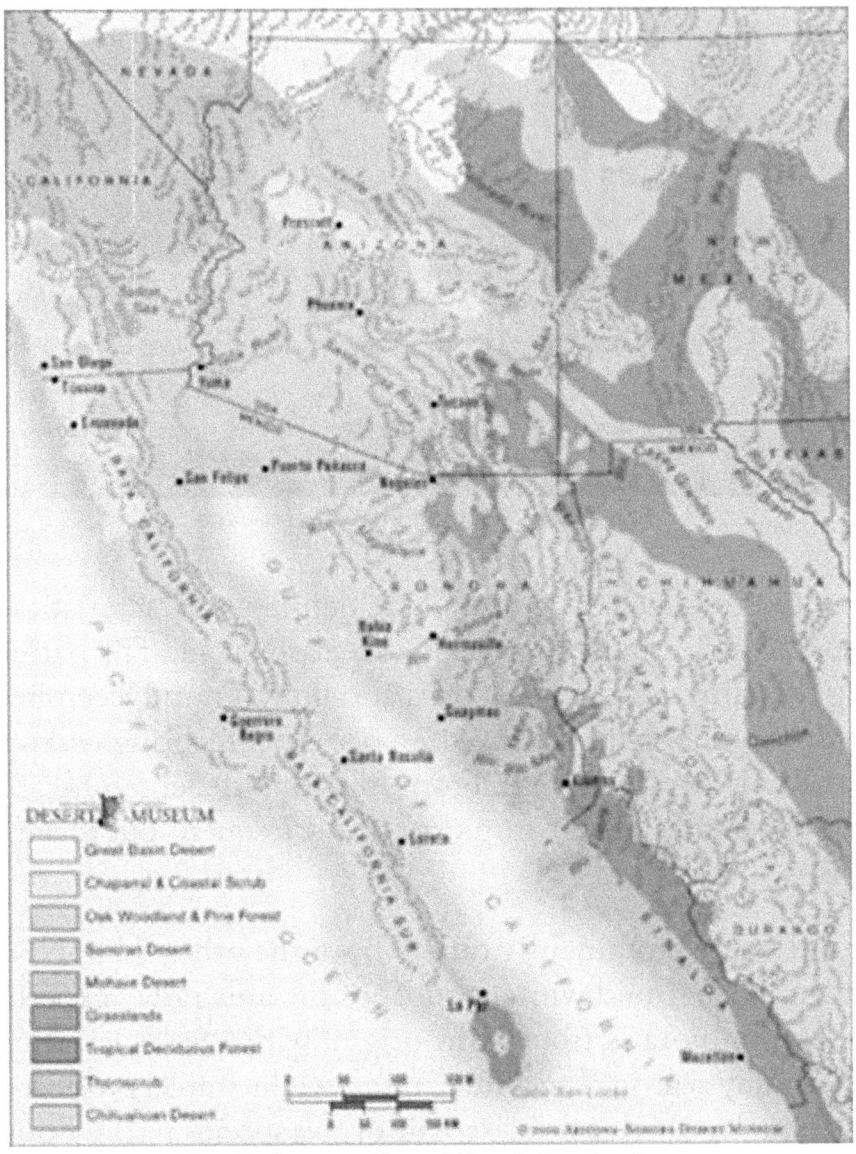

Fig. 23 Sonoran Desert Vegetative Regions

The Deserts of South America

South America has six deserts. The Atacama Desert **(Figure 24)** in Chile is considered the driest place on earth. The Patagonian Desert is Argentina's largest desert and the world's fourth most extensive desert.

Fig. 24 Atacama Desert

Patagonian Desert

This desert occupies an area of 259,846 square miles. A small section of the desert is part of the Chilean territory. The landscape of the Patagonian Desert **(Figure 25)** features alternating tablelands/massifs and canyons/valleys. In the western part of the steppe region of the desert, lakes of glacial origin dot the landscape. The notable fauna inhabiting the Patagonian Desert includes the lesser rhea, the Patagonian gray fox, western ribbon snake, the Patagonian weasel, guanaco, desert iguana and the burrowing owl.

Fig. 25 The Patagonian Desert

The Patagonian Desert is a place of ancient peoples and indigenous tribes. A place inhabited by dinosaurs more than 70 million years ago. Unlike what you may think, this is a cold place. In the desert of Eastern Patagonia, temperatures rarely exceed 54 degrees F and averages just 37 degrees F. The Patagonian Desert is a large cold winter desert. The region experiences about seven months of winter and five months of summer. Frost is not uncommon in the desert but, because of the very dry condition year round, snow is rare. The Andes, to the west of the desert, are the primary reason for the Patagonian desert status as they inhibit the westerly flow of moisture from the southern Pacific from reaching inland. This creates a rain shadow that accounts for the formation of the desert and is why, despite approximately half of the desert being only about 200 miles from the ocean; such a large desert is found in the region. The cold **Falkland Current** off the Atlantic coast of South America also contributes to the aridity of the area.

Atacama Desert

This desert, in northern Chile, is the driest place on the planet. The Atacama Desert **(Figure 26)** is on the other side of Eastern Patagonia. Therefore, you will find it is surrounded by the Andes in its eastern part and by the Pacific Ocean in the west. The Atacama Desert is known as the driest non-polar place in the world. It could be several years without rain in one of the largest deserts in South America.

Fig. 26 Atacama Desert 2

The Atacama Desert is one of the most notable deserts in South America occupying parts of Peru and Chile. It is an arid plateau, stretching along a length of 622 miles on the coast of the Pacific Ocean located to the west of the Andes mountains. The desert occupies an area of about 40,541 square miles. Large sections of the desert feature salt lakes, sand, **felsic lava**, and stony terrain. The Atacama Desert is known to be the world's driest non-polar location. In the central sector of the desert, rainfall often does not occur for periods of up to four or five years. The species diversity of the Atacama Desert is highly restricted. Some parts of the desert are too dry to sustain any life form at all. Scorpions, desert butterflies, and wasps, the Atacama toad, lava lizards and iguanas, are some of the Atacama Desert fauna. Birds visiting or residing in the desert include sparrows, hummingbirds, Andean flamingos and Humboldt penguins. Seals and sea lions can be sighted along the coast.

La Guajira Desert

The La Guajira Desert **(Figure 27)** is located in the northernmost part of Colombia, about 684 miles north of Bogota, the Capitol. The desert occupies most of the La Guajira Peninsula including some sections of Venezuelan territory. The peninsula is populated chiefly by **xeric scrubland,** which is home to a large variety of flora and fauna. The National Natural Park of Macuira, established in 1977, is a tropical oasis located in the La Guajira Desert. The park covers 62,000 acres in La Guajira's only mountain chain and ranges in elevation from sea level to 1,480 feet. It has a warm climate that averages about 81 degrees F. The region is rich in coal reserves and coal is mined in the El Cerrejon zone. The National Natural Park of Macuira is also located within the limits of the La Guajira Desert and represents a tropical oasis. A variety of desert flora and fauna inhabit the La Guajira Desert. The Wayuu people, an indigenous group of herders, also live in the desert habitat.

Fig. 27 The La Guajira Desert

Deserts of Asia

The Gobi Desert

The Gobi Desert **(Figure 28)** is the largest desert in Asia, covering 500,000 square miles. Extending from northern China into Mongolia, the Gobi Desert receives an average of 7 inches of rainfall each year because the Himalaya Mountains block rain clouds from reaching the region. The Silk Road actually passes through the Gobi Desert, and through historic trading cities such as Turfan, Hami and Dunhuang **(Side Bar P)**. Today, the Gobi continues to grow every year, as winds carry desert sand into nearby areas and erodes the surrounding top soil. This process of desertification renders fertile land unusable and occurs in the Gobi at an alarming rate for the nearby human population.

The Gobi is a rain shadow desert **(Figure 29)**, formed by the Tibetan Plateau blocking precipitation from the Indian Ocean reaching the Gobi territory. The Gobi measures over 1,000 miles from southwest to northeast and 500 miles from north to south. The desert is widest in the west, along the line joining the Lake Bosten and the Lop Nor (87°–89° east). It is the sixth-largest desert in the world and the second largest in Asia **(Side Bar Q)**. Much of the Gobi is not sandy but has exposed bare rock.

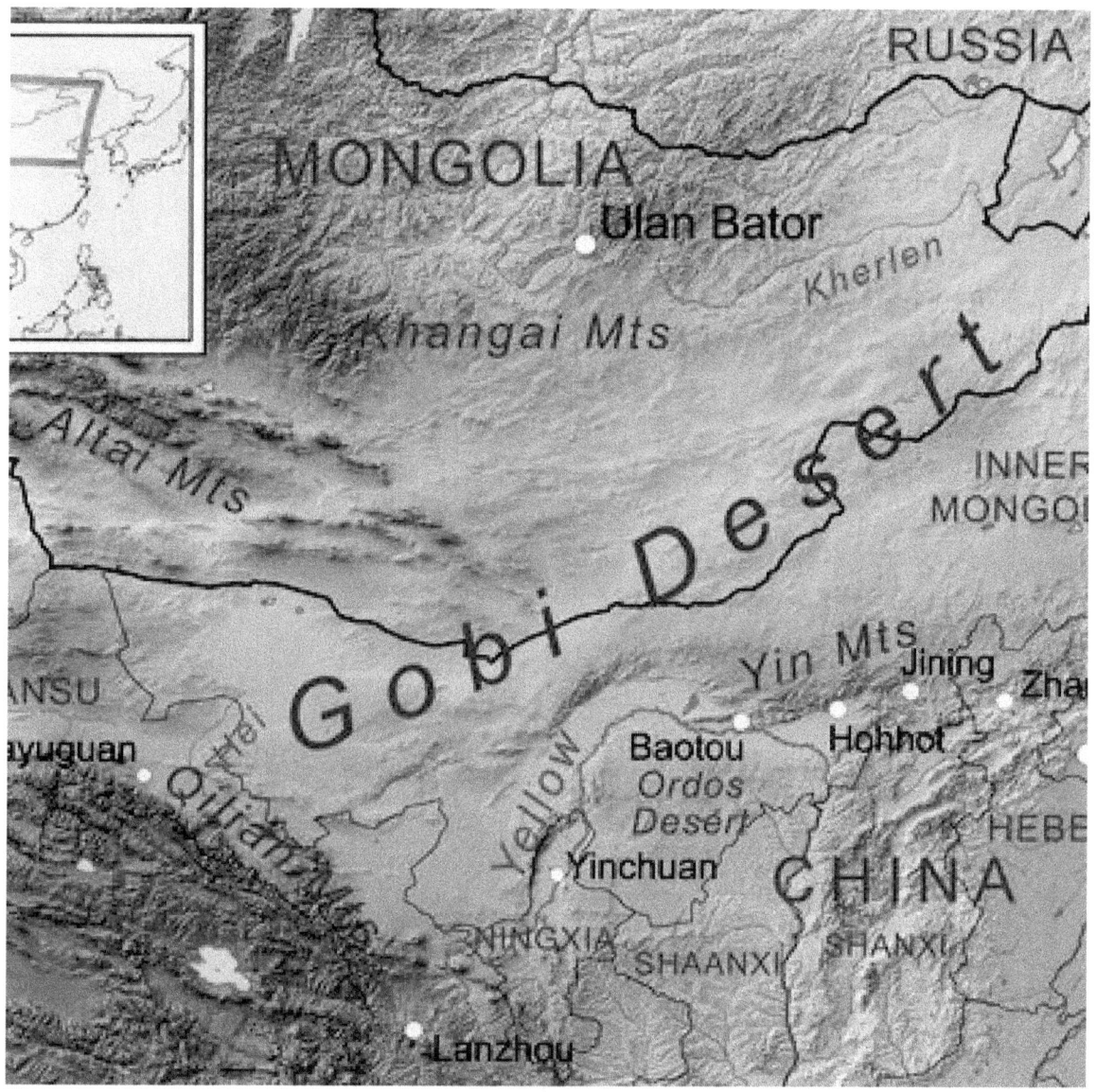
Fig. 28 Gobi desert map

Side Bar P Silk Roads

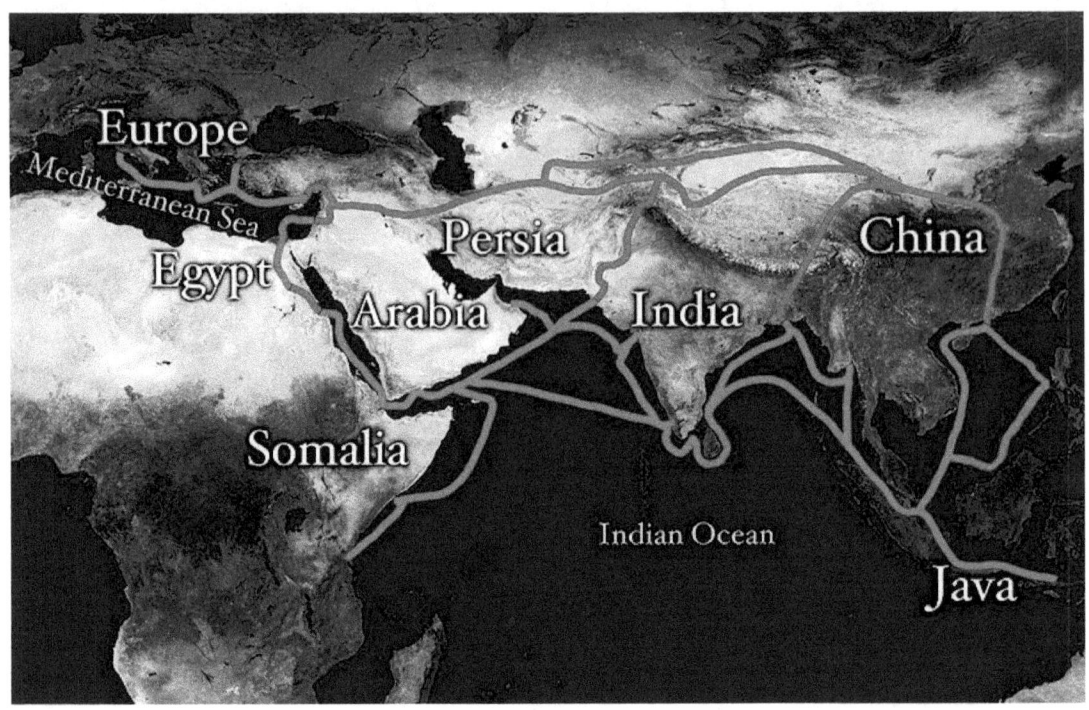

Fig. 29 Rain Shadow Effect

Side Bar Q 15 Facts about the Mongolian Gobi Desert

The **Gobi Desert** is the largest desert in Asia and fifth largest in the world. The desert stretches in two countries territory. It extends out to Mongolia's south and on the other side it reaches out to northern and northwestern parts of China. A Mongolian vast zone of desert and desert steppe covers almost thirty percent of the Mongolian territory.

People always imagine Gobi as a lifeless sandy desert. In reality, only five percent of the total area are sand dunes. The most of part of the Gobi Desert is a land of steppes, sands, mountains and it is the home for camel breeders, rich with wildlife and vegetation.

Gobi has one of the world's most extreme weather conditions with rapid temperature changes within a day and season.

Gobi holds the most important archaeological place where first discovered that Dinosaurs laid eggs. Gobi, which hid the dinosaur footprints until this time, came to the attention of the world attention this way.

You may think Gobi Desert does not have snowfall. It snows well enough to support its livestock and wild animals. Dunes of this area are covered with snow in winter.

The Gobi Desert is still growing as a result of climate change and desertification. Gobi camel herders are losing grassland.

The Gobi Desert has one of the most hospitable residents. Nomads always lack of visitors. Therefore, always welcome visitors pleasantly and give you food and lodging if you need it.

The animals living in the Gobi Desert are various. You can see bears, camels, golden eagles, gazelles, Kulan (*Equus hemionus*) and even snow leopards. Also, rodents include marmot and reptiles.

Gobi is not one thing—it comprises thirty-three areas with different features and climate. Gobi has canyons, flowery steppes, beautiful crags, wide hollows with few oases, saline and green saxaul thickets.

Mongolian Gobi Desert has one of the biggest and beautiful sand dunes called Khongoryn sand dune. It is 4-7 miles wide, 112 miles long and rising to a height of 260 feet maximum height to the apex can be 980 feet.

Ancient sub-species of the brown bear and only desert dwelling bear species, Mazaalai in Mongolian, (*Ursus arctos gobiensis*) lives in the Mongolian Gobi Desert. With less than thirty living individuals, the Gobi bear is on the brink of extinction. Mazaalai is the last preserved bear species that does not live in the zoo in other places

The Gobi Desert is one of the few areas, conserving the Bactrian camel (*Camelus bactrianus*) gene pool or Bactrian camel is native in the Gobi. According to the survey, almost seventy percent of the camel populations live in the Gobi Desert and semi desert regions.

The desert holds a very important historical place. The largest contiguous land empire of the world – the Great Mongolian Empire was flourishing in the Gobi Desert along the Silk Road.

The Gobi Desert is not only famous for dinosaur species discovery, but also well known for its rich natural resources. The Gobi Desert is rich in copper, gold and coal deposits. One of them is called Oyu Tolgoi which is world's third largest copper and gold mine.

Some geologists considered that Mongolian Gobi was once a bottom of sea in ancient time and found fossilized coral heads, 'sea lilies' and various shells in the Gobi Altai province.

The Gobi, broadly defined, can be divided into five distinct dry ecoregions, based on variations in climate and topography:

- **Eastern Gobi desert steppe, (Figure 30)** the easternmost of the Gobi ecoregions, covering an area of 108,804 square miles. It extends from the Inner Mongolian Plateau in China northward into Mongolia. It includes the Yin Mountains and many low-lying areas with salt pans and small ponds. It is bounded by the Mongolian-Manchurian grassland to the north, the Yellow River Plain to the southeast, and the Alashan Plateau semi-desert to the southeast and east.

Fig. 30 Eastern Gobi desert steppe

- **Alashan Plateau semi-desert (Figure 31; Side Bar R)** lies west and southwest of the Eastern Gobi desert steppe. It consists of the desert basins and low mountains lying between the Gobi Altai range on the north, the Helan Mountains to the southeast, and the Qilian Mountains and northeastern portion of the Tibetan Plateau on the southwest.

Fig. 31 Alashan Plateau semi-desert

Side Bar R Alashan Plateau semi-desert Map

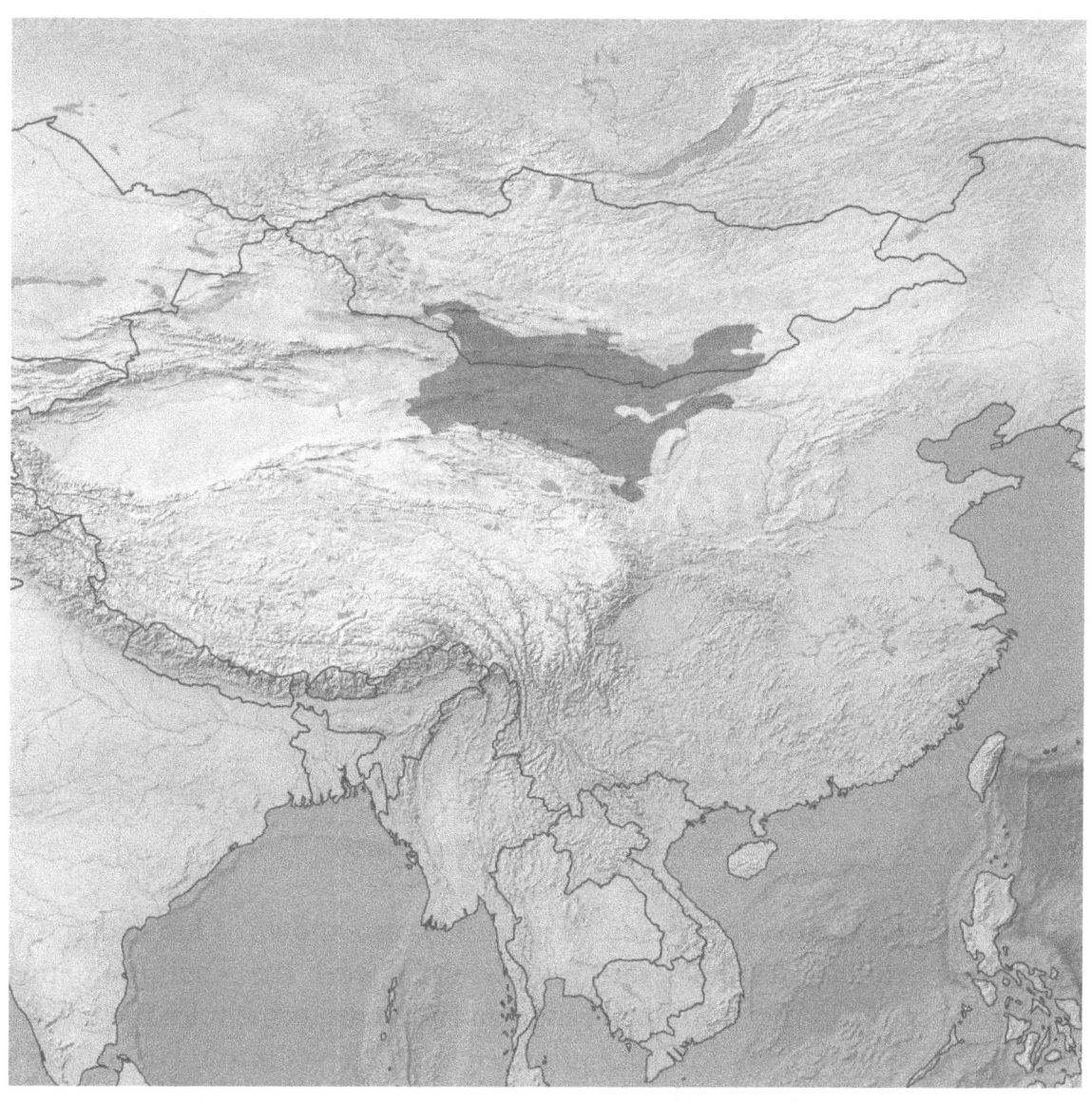

- **Gobi Lakes Valley desert steppe (Figure 32)** ecoregion lies north of Alashan Plateau semi-desert, between the Gobi Altai range to the south and the Khangai Mountains to the north.

Fig. 32 Gobi Lakes Valley desert steppe

- **Dzungarian Basin semi-desert (Figure 33)**, also known as Junggar Basin semi-desert, includes the desert basin lying between the Altai mountains on the north and the Tian Shan range on the south. It includes the northern portion of China's Xinjiang province and extends into the southeastern corner of Mongolia. The Alashan Plateau semi-desert lies to the east, and the Emin Valley steppe to the west, on the China-Kazakhstan border.

Fig. 33 Dzungarian Basin semi desert

- **Tian Shan range (Figure 34)**, The Tian Shan, meaning the *Mountains of Heaven* or the *Heavenly Mountain*, is a large system of mountain ranges located in Central Asia. The highest peak in the Tian Shan is Jengish Chokusu, at 24,406 feet high. Its lowest point is the Turpan Depression, which is 505 feet below sea level. These mountains separate the Dzungarian Basin semi-desert from the Takla Makan Desert, which is a low, sandy desert basin surrounded by the high mountain ranges of the Tibetan Plateau to the south and the Pamirs to the west. The Takla Makan Desert ecoregion includes the Desert of Lop.

Fig. 34 Central Tian Shan Mountains

Karakum Desert

Covering much of present-day Turkmenistan, the Karakum Desert **(Figure 35)** lies east of the Caspian Sea, with the Aral Sea to the north and the Amu Dar'ya River and the Kyzyl Kum desert to the northeast. In modern times, with the shrinking of the Aral Sea, the extended "Aral Karakum" has appeared on the former seabed, with an estimated area of 15,440 square miles. Although the level of the Aral Sea has fluctuated over its existence, the most recent level drop was caused by the former Soviet Union building massive irrigation projects in the region. Although the North Aral Sea is currently rising, the South Aral Sea is still dropping, thus expanding the size of the desert.

Fig. 35 Karakum Desert

The Karakum Desert is home to the Darvaza Gas Crater **(Figure 36)**. The Darvaza gas crater, also called the "Door to Hell" or the "Gates of Hell" by locals, is a crater of natural gas that has been burning since 1971. The crater is a major tourist attraction, with hundreds of visitors arriving each year.

Fig. 36 Darvaza Gas Crater

Takla Makan Desert (Figure 37)

The Takla Makan Desert adjoins the Gobi desert **(Figure 38)**. It is a low, sandy desert basin surrounded by the high mountain ranges of the Tibetan Plateau to the south and the Pamirs to the west. The Takla Makan Desert ecoregion includes the Desert of Lop **(Figure 39; Side Bar S)**.

Fig. 37 Takla Makan Desert

Fig. 38 The Gobi Desert

Fig. 39 Desert of Lop

Side Bar S Takla Makan Desert Map

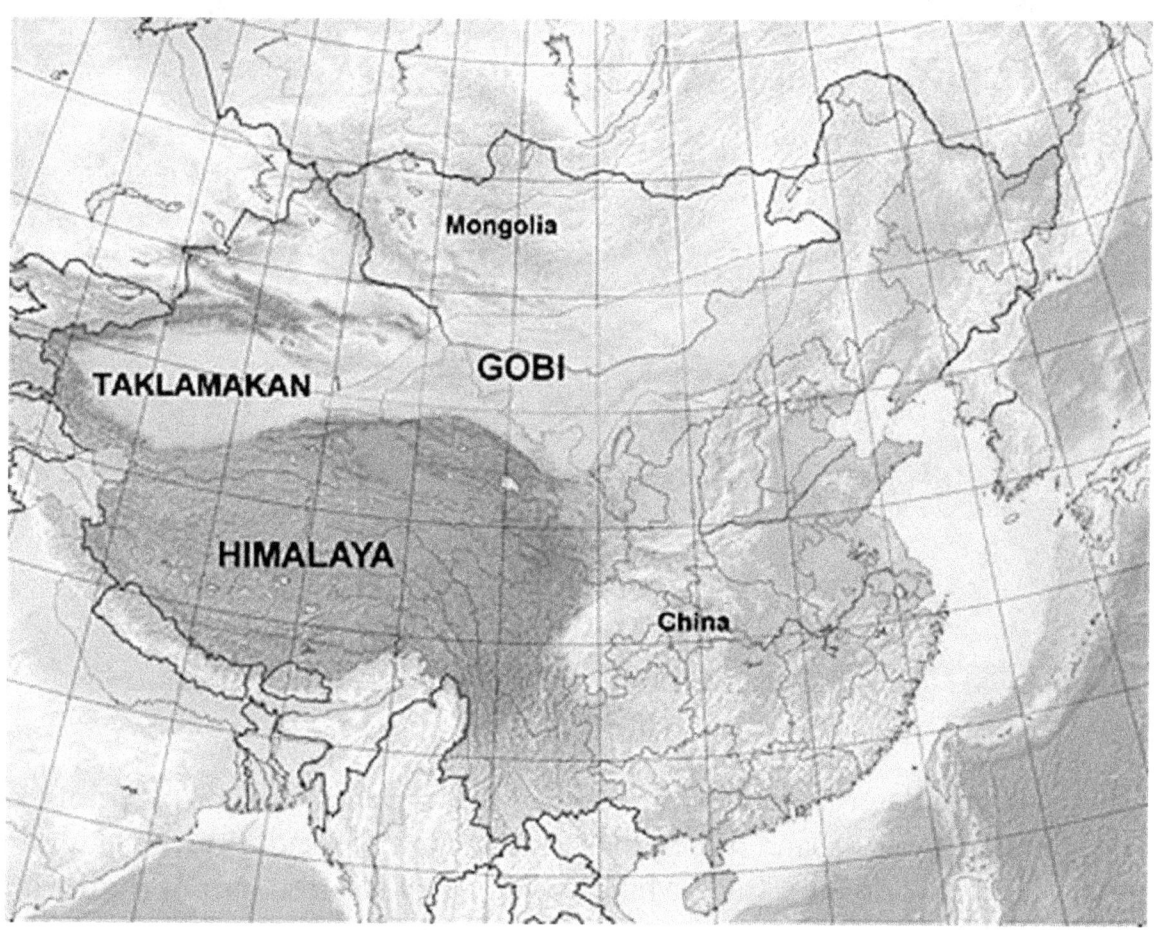

One of the world's largest deserts, the Takla Makan, is located in the northwest region of modern China, in Xinjiang Uighur Autonomous Region. There are oases located on two routes around the desert that served as important trading spots on the **Silk Road (Figure 40; Side Bar T)** Along the north, the route went by the Tien Shan Mountains and, along the south, the Kunlun Mountains of the Tibetan Plateau. Economist André Gunder Frank, who traveled along the northern route with the United Nations Educational, Scientific and Cultural Organization (UNESCO), says the southern route was most used in ancient times. It joined up with the northern route at Kashgar to head into India/Pakistan, Samarkand, and Bactria.

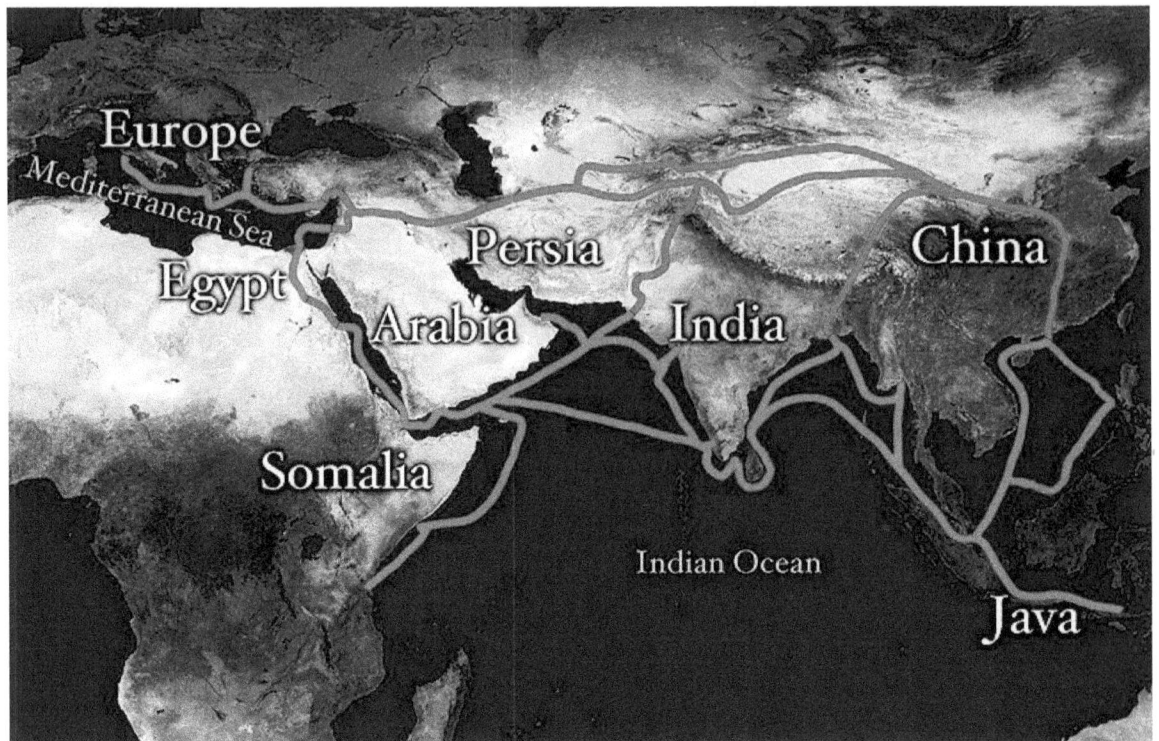

Fig. 40 The Silk Road

China's largest desert extends over 123,550 square miles. Composed primarily of shifting crescent sand dunes, the Takla Makan is one of the largest sandy deserts in the world. The Takla Makan occupies the central part of the Tarim Basin in the Uygur Autonomous Region of Xinjiang, western China. The desert area extends about 600 miles from west to east, and it has a maximum width of some 260 miles and a total area of approximately 123,550 square miles. The desert reaches elevations of 3,900 to 4,900 feet above sea level in the west and south and from 2,600 to 3,300 feet in the east and north.

Despite the inhospitable and unpredictable nature of the desert sands, the Chinese government erected a road across the desert in the mid-1990s.

Side Bar T More about the Silk Road

The Silk Road was an ancient trade route that linked the Western world with the Middle East and Asia. It was a major conduit for trade between the Roman Empire and China and later between medieval European kingdoms and China. Chinese merchants exported silk to Western buyers. From Rome and later from Christian kingdoms, wools, gold, and silver traveled eastward.

Apart from material goods, religion was one of the West's major exports along the Silk Road. Early Assyrian Christians took their faith to Central Asia and China, while merchants from the Indian subcontinent exposed China to Buddhism. Disease also traveled along the Silk Road. Many scholars believe that the bubonic plague was spread to Europe from Asia, causing the Black Death pandemic in the mid-14th century.

Parts of the Silk Road survive in the form of a paved highway connecting Pakistan and the Uyghur Autonomous Region of Xinjiang in China. In the 21st century the United Nations planned to sponsor a trans-Asian motor highway and railroad. The Silk Road also inspired China's Belt and Road Initiative, a global infrastructure development strategy authored by President and General Secretary Xi Jinping.

Deserts of Australia

Australia's ten deserts **(Figure 41)** are globally important arid lands with diverse habitats and significant natural features. The project area supports an exceptional range of animals and plants including numerous iconic threatened species, such as the bilby and rock wallaby. Indigenous Australians have inhabited the desert country for thousands of years and continue to have strong cultural and spiritual connections to the desert. The deserts span 104,248 square miles across five state and territory jurisdictions.

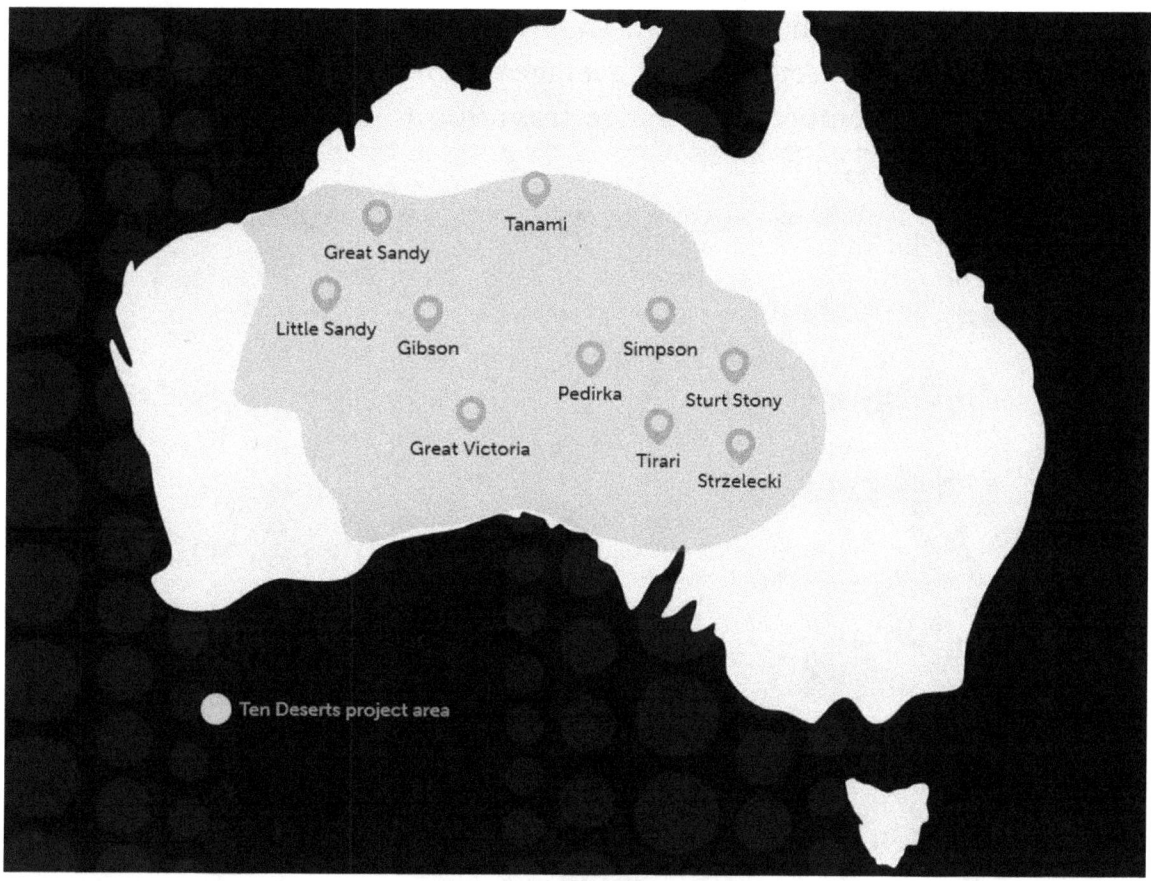

Fig. 41 Australia - 10 Deserts

Great Victoria Desert

The Great Victoria Desert **(Figure 42)** is the largest desert in Australia and consists of many small sandhills, grassland plains, areas with a closely packed surface of pebbles, called desert pavement or gibber plains, and salt lakes. It is over 430 miles wide (from west to east) and covers an area of 134,650 square miles, from the Eastern Goldfields region of Western Australia to the Gawler Ranges in South Australia. The Western Australian mulga shrublands ecoregion lies to the west, the Little Sandy Desert to the northwest, the Gibson Desert and the Central Ranges xeric shrublands to the north, the Tirari-Sturt stony desert to the east, while the Nullarbor Plain to the south separates it from the Southern Ocean. Average annual rainfall is low and irregular, ranging from 7.9 to 9.8 inches per year. Thunderstorms are relatively common in the Great Victoria Desert, with an average of 15–20 thunderstorms per year. Summer daytime temperatures range from 90o to 104o F, while in winter, this falls to 64o to 73o F.

Fig. 42 The Great Victoria Desert

Only the hardiest of plants can survive in much of this environment. Between the sand ridges there are areas of wooded steppe consisting of *Eucalyptus gongylocarpa*, *Eucalyptus youngiana* and mulga *(Acacia aneura)* shrubs scattered over areas of resilient spinifex grasses particularly *Triodia basedowii*.

Wildlife adapted to these harsh conditions includes few large birds or mammals. However, the desert does sustain many types of lizard including the vulnerable great desert skink (*Egernia kintorei*), the Central Ranges taipan discovered in 2007, and a number of small marsupials including the endangered sandhill dunnart *(Sminthopsis psammophila)* and the crest-tailed mulgara *(Dasycercus cristicauda)*. One way to survive here is to burrow into the sands, as a number of the desert animals, including the southern marsupial mole *(Notoryctes typhlops)*, and the water-holding frog do. Birds include the chestnut-breasted whiteface (*Aphelocephala pectoralis*) found on the eastern edge of the desert and the malleefowl of Mamungari Conservation Park. Predators of the desert include the dingo in that the desert is north of the Dingo Fence and two large monitor lizards, the perentie *(Varanus giganteus)* and the sand goanna *(Varanus gouldii)*.

As this area has had very limited use for agriculture, habitats remain largely undisturbed while parts of the desert are protected areas including Mamungari Conservation Park (formerly known as Unnamed Conservation Park) in South Australia, a large area of pristine arid zone wilderness which possesses cultural significance and is one of the fourteen World Biosphere Reserves in Australia. Habitat is also preserved in the large Aboriginal local government area of Anangu Pitjantjatjara Yankunytjatjara in South Australia and in the Great Victoria Desert Nature Reserve of Western Australia.

The nuclear weapons trials carried out by the United Kingdom at Maralinga and Emu Field in the 1950s and early 1960s have left areas contaminated with plutonium-239 and other radioactive material.

Great Sandy Desert

The Great Sandy Desert **(Figure 43)** is located across northwest and central Australia. It contains two of the country's most famous parks, the Rudall River National Park and Uluru-Kata Tjuta National Park where the famous Ayers Rock is located. It is the second largest desert in Australia after the Great Victoria Desert and encompasses an area of 110,036 sq miles. The Gibson Desert lies to the south and the Tanami Desert lies to the east of the Great Sandy Desert.

Fig. 43 Great Sandy Desert

Rainfall is low throughout the coast and far north and is strongly seasonal. Areas near the Kimberley have an average rainfall that exceeds 12 inches, but is patchy. Many drought years end with a monsoon cloud mass or tropical cyclone. Like many of Australia's deserts, rainfall is high by desert standards, with the driest parts recording falls little below 9.8 inches. A massive evaporation rate makes up for the higher than normal desert rainfall. This region is one which gives rise to the heat lows which help drive the NW monsoon. Almost all rain comes from monsoon thunderstorms or the occasional tropical cyclone rain depression. On average for most of the area, there are about 20–30 days where thunderstorms form; however, in the north bordering the Kimberley, 30-40 per year is the average.

Summer daytime temperatures are some of the hottest in Australia. The range on the northern border near the Kimberley at Halls Creek is around 99 to 100 degrees F, but this would be indicative of the low end of the range.

Regions further south average 100 to 108 degrees F, except when monsoonal cloud cover is active. Several people have died in this region after their vehicles broke down on remote tracks. Winters are short and warm; temperatures range from 77 to 86 degrees F.

Frost does not occur in most of the area. The regions bordering the Gibson Desert in the far southeast may record a light frost or two every year. Away from the coast winter nights can still be chilly in comparison to the warm days. The vegetation of the Great Sandy Desert is dominated by spinifex.

Animals in the region include feral camels, dingoes, goannas, including the large perentie, and numerous species of lizards and birds. Other animal inhabitants include bilbies, mulgara, marsupial moles, rufous hare-wallabies, thorny devils, bearded dragons, and red kangaroos.

Bird-life found within the desert includes the rare Alexandra's parrot, the mulga parrot and the scarlet-chested parrot.

The most striking features of the Great Sandy Desert include:

- Ergs or seas of sand that comprise linear, parallel dunes sculpted by winds blowing the same direction over a prolonged period. The dunes, covering much of the Big Sandy, extend for 25 to 30 miles or more in length, rise to 50 feet in elevation and trend west-northwest in orientation. From the air, the Great Sandy's ergs resemble immense furrowed fields **(Figure 44)**.

Fig. 44 Ergs of the Great Sandy Desert

- Kata Tjuta ("Many Heads" in the aboriginal language) that consist of some three dozen bald red sedimentary rock domes that tower above the desert floor in the southeastern part of the Great Sandy. Home to numerous mythical figures, the Kata Tjuta domes **(Figure 45)** have been sacred to various Aboriginal Australian tribes for perhaps 22,000 years.

Fig. 45 the Kata Tjuta domes

- Ayers Rock **(Figure 46)**, or Uluru, that ranks as the second largest monolith, or "island mountain," in the world, after Mount Augustus, also in Australia. Also sacred to the Aboriginals, Uluru, standing 1148 feet above the surrounding desert, stands as Australia's most iconic natural formation. It and Kata Tjuta serve as the central attractions for the country's Uluru-Kata Tjuta National Park.

Fig. 46 Ayres Rock

- Wolfe Creek Crater **(Figure 47)** that marks the site where a 55,000-ton asteroid, traveling 10 miles per second, struck some 300,000 years ago, according to the *Outback Australia Travel Guide*. The crater measures a half mile in diameter. Its rim rises some 80 feet above the surrounding desert. Its floor lies some 492 to 656 feet below the rim. Located in the transitional area between the Great Sandy and Tanami Deserts, in the north-central part of Australia, the crater is the principal feature of the Wolfe Creek National Park. According to Aboriginal beliefs, the crater marks the site where a rainbow serpent emerged from the ground.

Fig. 47 Wolfe Creek Meteorite Crater

IV. Plants and Animals in the Desert

The desert holds a place in the world as one of the most grueling terrains in existence. Although it may seem a lifeless place, there is no shortage of desert animals and plant—they are simply better adapted to the environment. Animals and plants range from large camels that have been utilized for transportation for centuries to trees that have evolved to survive on very little water. For desert plants and animals, information is abundant even if water is scarce.

The ability to adapt to arid conditions can mean the difference between life or death for animals and plants that live in the desert. Some animals burrow deep underground in the heat of the day then lie in the shade until late afternoon or early evening. Many have evolved salt glands, which allow their bodies to secrete salt but not sweat so they retain water. Most deserts have dry, arid climates with little to no rain, so every living organism that lives there must adapt, survive and thrive, or die.

Desert Plants

Most desert species have found remarkable ways to survive by evading drought. Desert succulents, such as cacti or rock plants (Lithops) for example, survive dry spells by accumulating moisture in their fleshy tissues. They have an extensive system of shallow roots to capture soil water only a few hours after it has rained. Additionally, many cacti and other stem-succulent plants of hot deserts present columnar growth, with leafless, vertically-erect, green trunks **(Side Bar U)** that maximize light interception during the early and late hours of the day, but avoid the midday sun, when excessive heat may damage plant tissues.

One of the most effective drought-survival adaptations for many species is the evolution of an ephemeral life-cycle. An ephemeral life cycle is characterized by a short life and the capacity to leave behind very hardy forms of propagation. This ability is found not only in plants but also in many invertebrates. Desert ephemerals are amazingly rapid growers capable of reproducing at a remarkably high rate during good seasons. These short-lived plants, usually ones that have one or more generations per year, growing only during favorable periods (as when adequate moisture is available) and passing the unfavorable periods in the form of seeds. The seed coats of some species contain a growth inhibitor that can be washed off only by a heavy rain, thus preventing **germination** after only a brief shower.

Some examples of desert plants include:

Desert Greasewood

The desert greasewood **(Figure 48)** or creosote bush (*Larrea tridentata*) adapted to life in the desert so well that there is one in California's Mojave Desert that is nearly 12,000 years old. The leaves contain a waxy substance that helps to keep out the sun's ultraviolet rays and preserve water, but once it does rain, the waxy material gives off a fragrance that many desert dwellers forever associate with the smell of rain. When a stem or branch of the plant dies, it sends up a new clone that grows in a circle surrounding the parent plant. Each part of the plant lives only about a century, but that cloning ability lets the entire plant structure stay alive for centuries.

Side Bar U About Desert Plants

Plant adaptations

Because of the dry climate, plants have developed a number of different methods of capturing water.

- Some plants have developed long (20-30 foot) taproots that go deep into the ground and tap into groundwater sources.

- Other plants have developed extensive horizontal root systems. These horizontal root systems lie just below the surface and extend far beyond the plant canopy. When it rains the numerous tiny roots capture the water.

- The mulga tree's root system lies close to the base of the tree. The tree survives because it has developed its own unique system of collecting water. The tree's numerous tiny leaves grow upward. When it rains the leaves capture the water and funnel it down along the branches to the center of the tree. The water then falls to the ground near the trunk of the tree where tree roots are concentrated/

Fig. 48 Desert greasewood

African Peyote Cactus

African Peyote Cactus **(Figure 49)** thrives in the desert environment. Its thick stems retain water for long periods of time. Its spiny leaves help prevent water loss because of evaporation. Native Saharan tribes use peyote from this plant in their spiritual rituals. Every time it rains, the African peyote cactus collects water, storing it in their thick stem and until it rains again, that is all they survive on. It lives with very little sun and prefers soil with a **pH** of 6 or 7. The plant can be started from seeds or the shoots of an older plant.

Fig. 49 African Peyote

Sahara lovegrass (Figure 50)

Fig. 50 Sahara lovegrass

Grasses are some of the toughest plants on earth, and lovegrass is no exception. This plant is widespread in the Sahara desert. It grows in tough clusters and produces small white flowers with edible seeds. Because lovegrass can grow back as long as its water-storing roots remain intact, it can survive in harsh desert conditions. The tangled roots also prevent soil erosion.

Date palm tree

Of all the trees in the Sahara desert, date palm trees **(Figure 51)** are the most useful to people. The fruits of this tree are used to sweeten beverages or are dried and eaten on their own. The leaves are sometimes used for food as well and can be tender and nutritious when cooked. Like the doum palm, date palms store water in their thick trunks, allowing them to survive in spite of the lack of rain in the Sahara.

Fig. 51 date palm tree

Mesquite tree

The mesquite tree **(Figure 52)** is one of the most common trees of the southwestern United States and parts of Mexico. It is a member of the legume family of plants which includes peanuts, alfalfa, clover, and beans. Perfectly adapted for its dry environment, the mesquite is a hardy tree. Here is the lowdown on the mesquite tree.

Fig. 52 Mesquite-tree

Palo verde tree

Palo verde trees **(Figure 53)** commonly occur in the Southwest: the foothill, yellow or littleleaf palo verde (*Parkinsonia aculeata*) and the blue palo verde (*Parkinsonia florida*). Palo verde – Spanish for green wood or stick – alludes to the plant's greenish branches and trunk. Common names refer to location, bark tints or comparative leaf size.

Fig. 53 Palo Verde Tree

Pods contain from one to eight seeds, with one being far more common than eight. The foothill species pods have narrow waists between the seeds, which are lentil sized. Blue palo verde seeds are slightly larger and flatter, with thicker, harder shells.

Both species are spiny, green, multi-trunked, deciduous trees. Foothill palo verdes only reach about 20 feet in height and have more yellowish bark and duller yellow/white flowers. Blue palo verdes top out at 40 feet. Their twigs and young branches are bluish-green, as are the leaves, which are larger than the foothill variety. Both have twice pinnate leaves (leaves with two stems and opposing leaflets on each stem), with the foothill species having more abundant leaves growing on longer stems.

The trees can photosynthesize through their green bark, an important adaptation for a tree that drops its leaves during the warm season and in response to fall cooling. Palo verdes also drop stems and branches to combat drought.

Palo verdes serve as nurse plants for saguaro cacti by providing a canopy – in effect, a microhabitat, which offers warmth in winter and shade in summer. The slower-growing, longer-lived cactus will eventually replace its one-time protector.

Bighorn sheep, mule deer, feral burros and jackrabbits as well as other small mammals browse palo verdes. Numerous birds forage, perch and/or nest in the abundant branches.

Desert Animals

Birds and large mammals can escape critical dry spells by migrating along the desert plains or up into the mountains. Smaller animals cannot migrate but regulate their environment by seeking out cool or shady places. In addition to flying to other habitats during the dry season, birds can reduce heat by soaring. Many rodents, invertebrates, and snakes avoid heat by spending the day in caves and burrows searching out food during the night. Animals active in the day reduce their activities by resting in the shade during the hotter hours.

When people think of a desert, often camels and rattle snakes spring to mind, however, many more animals call the desert home. Foxes, spiders, antelopes, elephants and lions are common desert species.

Some examples of desert animals include:

Fennec fox

The fennec fox **(Figure 54)** is found in the Sahara of North Africa, the Sinai Peninsula, South East Israel (Arava desert) and the Arabian Desert. Their large ears, which are usually 6 inches long, help dissipate excess body heat on hot days in the desert. The fennec fox seems to be the only carnivore living in the Sahara Desert able to survive without free water. Their kidneys are adapted to restrict water loss, their extensive burrowing may cause the formation of dew, which can then be consumed, and they will receive moisture from the food they eat. Their sandy fur helps to reflect heat, and also provides excellent camouflage. Their thick fur helps insulate them from the cold desert nights. Fennec foxes also have thick fur on the soles of their feet, also affords them excellent traction in the loose sand.

Fig. 54 Fennec Fox

Addax antelope

Male addax antelope **(Figure 55)** weigh from 220 to 300 pounds and have a shoulder height of 37–45 inches. Their horns are 30–43 inches long. Females are nearly as tall as males and only 10–20 percent lighter; their horns are thinner than the male's but just as long. A stocky build and sturdy, rather short legs give the addax endurance but not speed.

Fig. 55 Addux antelope

Other adaptations for desert life are developed to a high degree in the addax, including a highly reflective coat, an ability to extract all the water it needs from plants and to conserve that water by excreting dry feces and concentrated urine, and an ability to tolerate a rise of daytime body temperature by as much as 11degrees F before resorting to nasal panting to cool down. In the hottest weather, addaxes rest by day and feed at night and early morning when food plants have absorbed the maximum moisture from the air. The addax employs its short, blunt muzzle to graze coarse desert grasses, and when these are unavailable it browses on acacias, leguminous herbs, and water-storing plants such as melons and tubers.

Deathstalker Scorpion

The deathstalker scorpion **(Figure 56)** can be found in desert and scrubland habitats ranging from North Africa through to the Middle East. Its range covers a wide sweep of territory in the Sahara, Arabian Desert, Thar Desert, and Central Asia, from Algeria and Mali in the west through to Egypt, Ethiopia, Asia Minor and the Arabian Peninsula, eastward to Kazakhstan and western India in the northeast and southeast. Its habitat includes a diversity of terrains in arid and semi-arid zones with very high temperatures. They use burrows abandoned by other animals and spaces under debris, but they also dare to get inside homes.

Fig. 56 Deathstalker scorpion

Camel

Camels **(Figure 57)** are extremely well adapted to desert life. They have two rows of eyelashes to protect their eyes from the dust; they have fat in their hump so they can go days without food and they can even close their nostrils to stop from inhaling sand. When the camel exhales, water vapor becomes trapped in their nostrils and is reabsorbed into the body as a means to conserve water. Camels eating green herbage can ingest sufficient moisture in milder conditions to maintain the hydrated state of their bodies without the need for drinking.

Fig. 57 Camel

Camels do not directly store water in their humps; they are reservoirs of fatty tissue. Concentrating body fat in their humps minimizes the insulating effect fat would have if distributed over the rest of their bodies, helping camels survive in hot climates. When this tissue is metabolized, it yields more than one gram of water for every gram of fat processed. This fat metabolization, while releasing energy, causes water to evaporate from the lungs during respiration (as oxygen is required for the metabolic process): overall, there is a net decrease in water.

Thorny devil (Figure 58)

Fig. 58 thorny devil

The thorny devil (**Side Bar V**) grows up to 8.3 inches in total length, which includes the tail and can live for 15 to 20 years. The females are larger than the males. Most specimens are colored in camouflaging shades of desert browns and tans. These colors change from pale colors during warm weather to darker colors during cold weather. The thorny devil is covered entirely with conical spines that are mostly uncalcified.

The thorny devil usually lives in the arid scrubland and desert that covers most of central Australia, sandplain and sandridge desert in the deep interior and the mallee belt. The habitat of the thorny devil coincides more with the regions of sandy loam soils than with a particular climate in Western Australia.

Side Bar V Fun Facts about the thorny devil

- The names given to Thorny devils reflect their appearance: the two large horned scales on their head complete the illusion of a dragon or devil. The name Moloch was used for a deity of the ancient Near East, usually depicted as a hideous beast. Thorny devils also have other nicknames people have given them such as the "devil lizard", "horned lizard", and the "thorny toad".

- Thorny devils have ridged scales that allow the animals to collect water by simply touching it with any part of the body, usually the limbs; the capillary principle allows the water to be transported to the mouth through the skin. And in extreme circumstances, Thorny devils may simply bury themselves in the sand and get moisture from it.

- Thorny devils have a very unusual gait; it involves freezing and rocking as the animal moves about slowly in search of food, water, or mates.

- Thorny devils can eat up to 3,000 ants at a time.

- Thorny devils can inflate their chests with air to appear bigger for predators and scare them as it makes it harder to swallow them.

Rockhopper penguin (*Eudyptes chrysocome*)

Rockhopper penguins **(Figure 59)** are among the smaller species of penguin. They range from 3 inches to 6 where males are larger than females. Afeeter reaching full growth, they are about 20 inches in height. Males and females cannot be distinguished just by looks, so a DNA test is conducted by taking a feather from the bird to determine its gender. Like many penguins, the rockhopper penguin has a white belly and the rest of its body is black.

Fig. 59 Rockhopper penguin

As other penguins, rockhoppers have a layered defense against the cold. They have a substantial layer of fat, followed by a layer of down on their skin that keeps heat in. In addition to that, they have a mesh of tightly overlapping waterproof feathers. Penguins have the highest number of feathers of any birds – sometimes up to 12 per 1/3 inch. Rockhopper Penguins generally live about 10 years in the wild.

Sand cat (*Felis margarita*)

The sand cat **(Figure 60)** is the only cat living chiefly in true deserts. This small cat is widely distributed in the deserts of North Africa, the Middle East and Central Asia. Owing to long hairs covering the soles of its feet, the sand cat is well adapted to the extremes of a desert environment and tolerant of extremely hot and cold temperatures. It inhabits both sandy and stony deserts, in areas far from water sources.

Fig. 60 Sand cat

Sand cats have dense hair and pads on the soles of each foot that protect against the intense heat and cold of their habitat, as well as aiding in movement across the sand. The pads help them navigate across shifting sands. Sand cats are fearless snake hunters—their prey can include venomous vipers and other snakes.

Saharan horned viper (*Cerastes cerastes*)

The horned desert viper **(Figure 61)** is a venomous species of viper native to the deserts of northern Africa and parts of the Middle East. It ofeeten is easily recognized by the presence of a pair of supraocular "horns", although hornless individuals do occur. These snakes favor dry, sandy areas with sparse rock outcroppings, and tend not to prefer coarse sand. Occasionally, they are found around oases, and up to an altitude of 4,900 feet. Cooler temperatures, with annual averages of 68° F or less, are preferred.

Fig. 61 Saharan horned viper

They typically move about by sidewinding, during which they press their weight into the sand or soil, leaving whole-body impressions. Often, it is even possible to use these impressions to make ventral scale counts. They have a reasonably placid temperament, but if threatened, they may assume a C-shaped posture and rapidly rub their coils together. Because they have strongly **keeled scales**, this rubbing produces a rasping noise, similar to the sound produced by snakes of the genus *Echis*, which have a characteristic threat display, rubbing sections of their body together to produce a "sizzling" warning sound. In the wild, they are typically ambush predators, lying submerged in sand adjacent to rocks or under vegetation. When approached, they strike very rapidly, holding on to the captured prey (small birds and rodents) until the venom takes effect.

Mazaalai (The Gobi bear) (Figure 62)

Fig. 62 The mazaalai

The Gobi bear (*Ursus arctos gobiensis*) is a subspecies of the brown bear (*Ursus arctos*) that is found in the Gobi Desert of Mongolia. It is listed as critically endangered by the Mongolian Redbook of Endangered Species and by IUCN standards. Recent surveys documented just 51 bears in 2022, a slight increase from an estimate of 40 bears in 2017. Gobi bears are separated by enough distance from other brown bear populations to achieve reproductive isolation. In 1959, hunting of the animal was prohibited to preserve the dying subspecies.

Baer's pochard (Figure 63)

Fig. 63 Baer's pochard

This species is classified as Critically Endangered as it is apparently undergoing an extremely rapid population decline, as measured by numbers on both the breeding and wintering grounds. It is now absent or occurs in extremely reduced numbers over the majority of its former breeding and wintering grounds and is common nowhere. It is thought that wetland destruction and over-harvesting of both birds and eggs are the key reasons for its decline. **Population size:** 150-700; **Population trend:** Decreasing.

Mongolian ground jay (Figure 64)

Fig. 64 Mongolian ground jay

Mongolian ground jay *(Podoces hendersoni)* can be found in arid areas of Central Asia (Mongolia, northern China and adjacent areas of Russia and Kazakhstan). Females spend more time foraging and the males spend more time brooding the chicks at the start of the nesting period. The main diet of the nestling Mongolian ground jay consists of common lizards, toad-headed agama, and invertebrates. It is thought Mongolian ground jays feed their chicks based on the availability of their food rather than in relation to the stage of the chicks' development.

It is listed as "Least concern" globally under the IUCN Red List of Threatened Species, but holds a regional status of "Vulnerable" with less than 10,000 individuals in Mongolia.

Pallas's sandgrouse (Figure 65)

Fig. 65 Pallas's sandgrouse

Pallas's sandgrouse *(Syrrhaptes paradoxus)* is 12–16 inches long with small, pigeon-like head and neck, but sturdy compact body. It has long pointed wings and tail and legs and toes are feathered. Its plumage is buff-colored, barred above with a black belly patch and pale underwings. The black belly and pale underwing distinguish this species from the related Tibetan sandgrouse. The male Pallas's sandgrouse is distinguished by its grey head and breast, orange face and grey breast band. The female has duller plumage and lacks the breast band though it has more barring on the upperparts.

The small feet lack a hind toe, and the three front toes are fused together. The upper surface is feathered, and the underneath has a fleshy pad. The appearance of the foot is more like a paw than an avian foot.

Related to their primarily dry diet of seeds, the sandgrouse needs to drink a large volume of water. The sandgrouse's wing morphology allows for fast flight with speeds up to 40 mph having been recorded. Large flocks of several thousand individuals fly to watering holes at dawn and dusk making round trips of up to 75 miles per day. Male parents soak their breast plumage in water while drinking, allowing their chicks to drink from the absorbed moisture on their return.

V. Peoples of the Desert

Despite the desert being so inhospitable, there are ethnic groups living in these places; they are groups of people that have to keep moving in caravans in search of places with water and food, defying the greatest risks: sandstorms, silted up wells and loss of bearings because of the lack of points of references. Some of these peoples are the Berbers of North Africa, which include the Kabyles and the Tuaregs; the Bedouins of the Arabic deserts; the Bejas in Namibia; the Sāns in the Kalahari desert and the Australian Aborigines.

Berbers of North Africa

Berbers are an ethnic group of several nations mostly indigenous to North Africa and some northern parts of West Africa. Berbers constitute the populations of Morocco, Algeria, Tunisia, Libya, Mauritania, northern Mali, northern Niger, and a small part of western Egypt.

Berber nations **(Side Bar W)** are distributed over an area stretching from the Atlantic Ocean to the Siwa Oasis in Egypt and from the Mediterranean Sea to the Niger River in West Africa. Historically, Berber nations spoke the Berber language, which is a branch of the Afroasiatic language family. The Berbers of Algeria were independent of outside control during the period of Ottoman Empire rule in North Africa. They lived primarily in three different Nations: the Kingdom of Ait Abbas, Kingdom of Kuku, and the principality of Aït Jubar. Kingdom of Ait Abbas is a Berber nation of North Africa, controlling Lesser Kabylie and its surroundings from the sixteenth century to the nineteenth century. It is referred to in the Spanish historiography as "reino de Labes"; sometimes more commonly referred to by its ruling family, the Mokrani, in Berber *At Muqran*, in Arabic *Ouled Moqrane*. Its capital was the Kalâa of Ait Abbas, an impregnable citadel in the Biban mountain range.

There are about 32 million Berbers in North Africa who still speak the Berber language, most living in Morocco, Algeria, Libya, Tunisia, northern Mali, and northern Niger. Smaller Berber-speaking populations are also found in Mauritania, Burkina Faso and Egypt's Siwa town. The majority of North

Side Bar W Berbers in North Africa

Throughout history, North Africa's native Berber-speaking populations have been central to the mix of political, social, cultural, and linguistic attributes that rendered the region distinct. At the dawn of the 20th century, Berbers still constituted a substantial majority of sharifian Morocco's population, and a significant minority of French Algeria's Muslim populace; their numbers were smaller in Ottoman Libya and smaller still in France's Tunisian protectorate.

Nationalism began to spread in North Africa during the first decades of the 20th century. Each nationalist movement was shaped by a particular combination of factors; all of them, however, foregrounded the Arab and Islamic components of their collective identities, downplaying or ignoring the Berber ones.

Berbers actively participated in the struggles for independence in both Algeria and Morocco, often in leadership roles. This pattern would continue during the decades after independence, even as the Algerian and Moroccan states placed supreme value on the Arabization of the educational system, and of public life in general. The state's overall view of Berber identity was that it should be consigned to the realm of folklore.

Even as the number of Berber speakers continued to decline, however, there arose a modern Berber (Amazigh) identity movement that demanded a re-examination of the underlying bases of their countries' collective identities, one that would bring the Berber language and culture to center stage. It also demanded genuine amelioration of the dire conditions of poverty that characterized much of the rural Berber world. As ruling regimes struggled to maintain their legitimacy after a half century of independence, the Berber "question" now took on a new salience in North Africa's increasingly contested political space.

Africa's population west of Egypt is believed to be Berber in ethnic origin, although because of Arabization and Islamization, some ethnic Berbers identify as Arabized Berbers. There are large immigrant Berber communities living in France, Spain, Canada, Belgium, the Netherlands, United Kingdom, Italy and other countries of Europe.

The majority of Berbers are Sunni Muslim. The Berber identity is usually wider than language and ethnicity and encompasses the entire history and geography of North Africa. Berbers are not an entirely **homogeneous** ethnicity, and they encompass a range of societies, ancestries and lifestyles. The unifying forces for the Berber people may be their shared language or a collective identification with Berber heritage and history.

Kabyle

The Kabyle people **(Side Bar X)** are a Berber ethnic group indigenous to Kabylia in the north of Algeria, spread across the Atlas Mountains, one hundred miles east of Algiers. They represent the largest Berber-speaking population of Algeria and the second largest in North Africa.

Many of the Kabyle have emigrated from Algeria, influenced by factors such as the Algerian Civil War, cultural repression by the central Algerian government, and overall industrial decline. Their **diaspora** has resulted in Kabyle people living in numerous countries. Large populations of Kabyle people settled in France and, to a lesser extent, Canada.

Side Bar X The Kabyle People

The Kabyle are Berbers located in the coastal mountain regions of northern Algeria. The Arabs call this entire region of North Africa "Maghrib". The Maghrib was conquered by the Muslims between 670 and 700. "Berber" comes from an Arabic name for the aboriginal people west and south of Egypt.

Tuaregs

The epitome of life in the desert are the Tuaregs **(Figure 66)**, who for centuries have spent their lives riding their dromedaries along the Saharan tracks. Also called the "blue men" **(Side Bar Y)** for the typical veils they wear to protect themselves from the sand and the heat, these people live in camps of tents built of dozens of goatskins painted in red ochre and skillfully sown together by their women to guard all the items and tools of everyday life. The Tuaregs mainly live on products derived from their animals. Their foods are curdled milk, fermented butter, dates and cereals (millet in particular) from which they make flour. They rarely eat meat, but when they have guests they just have to honor them so they kill a goat according to Muslim traditions. Water is carried in scooped-out and sun-dried pumpkins, whose decorated surfaces hint at the groups who produced them. Originally, the Tuaregs were a nomadic people, but later many conflicts and French colonization pushed many of them to lead a **sedentary** life and the few nomadic ones that have been lefeet live on the products of their animals and other foodstuffs they obtain through trade and breed horses and dromedaries.

Fig. 66 Tuareg woman

They produce handicrafts, for instance engraved silverware; they tan hides, make mats and produce rugs and textiles out of dromedary wool. Farming as well as high-level handicrafts are produced by lower castes, who live sedentarily in the oases. Today, some Tuaregs have found employment in the service sector, especially tourism, because they know the desert so well, they work as tour guides.

Side Bar Y The Blue Men

The Tuaregs have been called the "blue people" for the indigo dye colored clothes they traditionally wear and which stains their skin. A semi-nomadic Muslim people, they are believed to be descendants of the Berber natives of North Africa. The Tuareg have been one of the ethnic groups that have been influential historically in the spread of Islam and its legacy in North Africa and the adjacent Sahel region.

The Bedouins

The Bedouin or Bedu **(Side Bar Z)** are a grouping of nomadic Arab people who have historically inhabited the desert regions in North Africa, the Arabian Peninsula, Iraq and the Levant. The English word *bedouin* comes from the Arabic *badawī*, which means "desert dweller", and is traditionally contrasted with *ḥāḍir*, the term for sedentary people. Bedouin territory stretches from the vast deserts of North Africa to the rocky sands of the Middle East. They are traditionally divided into tribes, or clans, and historically share a common culture of herding camels and goat. The vast majority of Bedouin adhere to Islam, although there are some fewer numbers of Arab Christian Bedouins present in the Fertile Crescent.

While many Bedouins have abandoned their nomadic and tribal traditions for a modern urban lifestyle, many retain traditional Bedouin culture such as retaining the traditional clan structure, traditional music, poetry, dances (such as *saas*), and many other cultural practices and concepts. Urbanized Bedouins often organize cultural festivals, usually held several times a year, in which they gather with other Bedouins to partake in and learn about various Bedouin traditions—from poetry recitation and traditional sword dances to playing traditional instruments and even classes teaching traditional tent knitting. Traditions like camel riding and camping in the deserts are still popular leisure activities for urbanized Bedouins who live in close proximity to deserts or other wilderness areas.

Livestock and herding, principally of goats, sheep and dromedary camels comprised the traditional livelihoods of Bedouins. These were used for meat, dairy products, and wool. Most of the staple foods that made up the Bedouins' diet were dairy products.

Camels, in particular, had numerous cultural and functional uses. Having been regarded as a "gift from God", they were the main food source and method of transportation for many Bedouins. In addition to their extraordinary milking potentials under harsh desert conditions, their meat was occasionally consumed by Bedouins. As a cultural tradition, camel races were organized during celebratory occasions, such as weddings or religious festivals

Side Bar Z The Bedouin

Bedouin, also spelled Beduin, Arabic Badawi and plural Badw, Arabic-speaking nomadic peoples of the Middle Eastern deserts, especially of North Africa, the Arabian Peninsula, Egypt, Israel, Iraq, Syria, and Jordan.

The Bejas

Beja **(Side Bar AA),** Arabic Bujah, nomadic people grouped into tribes and occupying mountain country between the Red Sea and the Nile and Atbara rivers from the latitude of Aswān southeastward to the Eritrean Plateau—that is, from southeastern Egypt through Sudan and into Eritrea. Numbering about 1.9 million in the early 21st century, the Beja are descended from peoples who have lived in the area since 4000 BCE or earlier.

The Beja people are ethnic Cushitic peoples inhabiting Sudan, Egypt, and Eritrea. In recent history, they have lived primarily in the Eastern Desert. They number around 1,237,000 people. Majority of Beja people speak the Beja language as a mother tongue, which belongs to the Cushitic branch of the Afro-Asiatic family. In Eritrea and southeastern Sudan, many members of the Beni Amer grouping speak Tigre. While many secondary sources identify the Ababda as an Arabic-speaking Beja tribe because of their cultural links with the Bishaari, this is a misconception: The Ababda do not consider themselves Beja, nor are they so considered by other Beja peoples.

The Beja people inhabit a general area between the Nile River and the Red Sea in Sudan, Eritrea and eastern Egypt known as the Eastern Desert. Most of them live in the Sudanese states of Red Sea around Port Sudan, River Nile, Al Qadarif and Kassala, as well as in Northern Red Sea, Gash-Barka, and Anseba Regions in Eritrea, and southeastern Egypt. There are smaller populations of other Beja ethnic groups further north into Egypt's Eastern Desert.

Some Beja groups are nomadic. The Kharga Oasis in Egypt's Western Desert is home to a large number of Qamhat Bisharin who was displaced by the Aswan High Dam. Jebel Uweinat is revered by the Qamhat.

Side Bar AA The Beja People

Most of the Beja prefer to live apart from their neighbors, and many are said to be indifferent to trade and modernization. Essentially **pastoralists**, the Beja move over vast distances with their flocks and herds of cattle and camels on whose produce—milk, butter, and meat—they subsist almost entirely.

The Sāns

The Sān or Saan peoples **(Figure 67)**, also known as the "Bushmen", are members of various Khoesān-speaking indigenous hunter-gatherer groups that are the first nations of Southern Africa, and whose territories span Botswana, Namibia, Angola, Zambia, Zimbabwe, Lesotho and South Africa. There is a significant linguistic difference between the northern peoples living between the Okavango River in Botswana and Etosha National Park in northwestern Namibia, extending up into southern Angola; the central peoples of most of Namibia and Botswana, extending into Zambia and Zimbabwe; and the southern people in the central Kalahari towards the Molopo River, who are the last remnant of the previously extensive indigenous Sān of South Africa.

The ancestors of the hunter-gatherer Sān are thought to have been the first inhabitants of what is now Botswana and South Africa. The historical presence of the San in Botswana is particularly evident in the Tsodilo Hills region of northern Botswana. In this area, stone tools and rock art paintings date back over 70,000 years and are by far the oldest known art. Sān was traditionally semi-nomadic, moving seasonally within certain defined areas based on the availability of resources such as water, game animals, and edible plants. As of 2010, the Sān populations in Botswana number about 50,000 to 60,000.

Fig. 67 Saans People

From the 1950s through to the 1990s, Sān communities switched to farming because of government-mandated modernization programs. Despite the lifestyle changes, they have provided a wealth of information in anthropology and genetics. One broad study of African genetic diversity completed in 2009 found that Sān people were among the five populations with the highest measured levels of genetic diversity among the 121 distinct African populations sampled. Certain Sān groups are one of 14 known extant "ancestral population clusters". That is, groups of populations with common genetic ancestry, who share ethnicity and similarities in both their culture and the properties of their languages.

Australian Aborigines

Aboriginal Australians **(Figure 68)** are the various **Indigenous** peoples of the Australian mainland and many of its islands, such as Tasmania, Fraser Island, Hinchinbrook Island, the Tiwi Islands and Groote Eylandt, but excluding the Torres Strait Islands. Aboriginal Australians comprise many distinct peoples that have developed across Australia for over 50,000 years. A new genomic study has revealed that Aboriginal Australians are the oldest known civilization on Earth, with ancestries stretching back roughly 75,000 years.

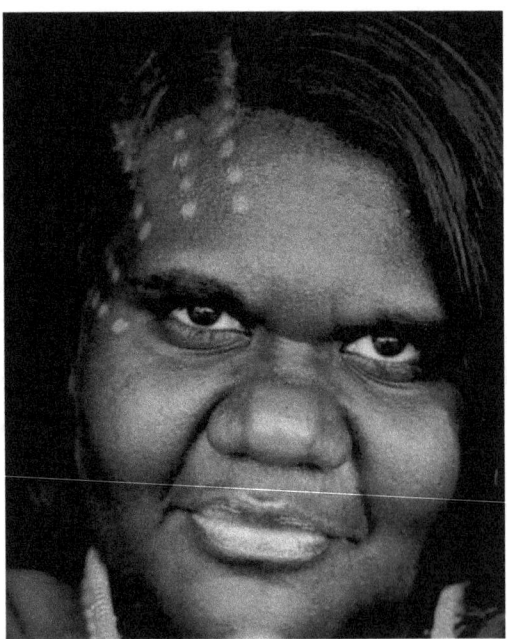

Fig. 68 Aboriginal woman

These peoples have a broadly shared, though complex, genetic history, but it is only in the last two hundred years they have been defined and started to self-identify as a single group. The definition of the term "Aboriginal" has changed over time and place, with the importance of family lineage, self-identification and community acceptance all being of varying importance.

The term 'Indigenous Australians' refers to Aboriginal Australians as well as Torres Strait Islanders, and the term should only be used when both groups are included in the topic being addressed or by self-identification by a person as Indigenous. Torres Strait Islanders are ethnically and culturally distinct, despite extensive cultural exchange with some of the Aboriginal groups, and the Torres Strait Islands are mostly part of Queensland but have a separate governmental status.

In the past, Aboriginal Australians lived over large sections of the continental shelf and were isolated on many of the smaller offshore islands and Tasmania when the land was inundated at the start of the Holocene inter-glacial period, about 11,700 years ago. Studies regarding the genetic makeup of Aboriginal groups are still ongoing, but evidence has suggested they have genetic inheritance from ancient Asian but not more modern peoples, share some similarities with Papuans, but have been isolated from Southeast Asia for a very long time. Before extensive European settlement, there were over 250 Aboriginal languages.

As of 2016, Aboriginal Australians comprised 3.1 percent of the population of Australia. They also live throughout the world as part of the Australian diaspora. Most Aboriginal people speak English, with Aboriginal phrases and words being added to create Australian Aboriginal English, which also has a tangible influence of Indigenous languages in the phonology and grammatical structure. They have a number of health and economic deprivations in comparison with the wider Australian community.

Aboriginal Australians possess inherited abilities to stand a wide range of environmental temperatures in various ways. A 1958 study comparing cold adaptation in the desert-dwelling Pitjantjatjara people compared to a group of white people showed the cooling adaptation of the Aboriginal group differed from that of the white people, and they were able to sleep more soundly through a cold desert night. A 2014 Cambridge University study found a beneficial mutation in two genes which regulate thyroxine, a hormone involved in regulating body metabolism, helps to regulate body temperature in response to fever. The effect of this is the desert people are able to have a higher body temperature without accelerating the activity of the whole of the body, which can be especially detrimental in childhood diseases. This helps people survive the side-effects of infection.

Natives of the North American Deserts

As ancient dwellings, rock paintings and carvings, and other archaeological remains testify, desert-culture Indians had developed a distinctive way of life within the approximate boundaries of the North American Desert thousands of years before the coming of Europeans **(Side Bar BB)**. Spanish explorers were the first Europeans to penetrate the southwestern area, and their legacy has molded much of the character of the region. It was only in the 19th century that a great wave of settlement, often attracted by the lure of mineral wealth, primarily gold and silver, swept westward over the whole area on its way to the more fertile regions of the Pacific coast; lefeet behind was a scattering of settlements focused on mineral wealth and irrigated regions and, even more sparsely, in the vast areas given over to sheep and cattle grazing.

Large areas of the contemporary landscape are occupied by Indian reservations **(Figure 69)**, a legacy of America's continental expansion. Military installations, some associated with past testing of nuclear weapons, also take up vast areas. The various types of agriculture encompass dryland farming, sheep and cattle grazing, and more intensive developments on irrigated oases. Mineral exploitation has continued, often to the detriment of the natural environment, and manufacturing has become associated with growing urban settlement in the more favored regions. Air pollution, caused by the burning of fossil fuels in population centers along the Pacific coast as well as in the interior, now reaches the most remote areas of the desert. Tourism also has grown immensely. Many areas near urban centers now support luxurious golf

Side Bar BB Facts about Southwest American Indian Tribes

- The Indians of this region generally lived in a harsh and inhospitable environment. Most of the region is hot and rocky and receives very little rainfall. There are some forests in the higher elevations and a few river valleys.

- Most of the Indians of Southwest America including the Hopi, Yuam, and Zuni tribes were traditionally farmers and lived in permanent homes. Because of the harsh environment, farming was challenging and usually required irrigation.

- Some of the tribes in this region, including the Apache and Navajo were nomadic hunters.

- Turquoise is used extensively in Southwest Indian jewelry. The Indians believe turquoise promotes happiness, health, and good fortune.

- The Indians of the southwest are famous for their beautiful traditional baskets. These baskets are colorful and have beautiful patterns. The indigenous people of this region have been using the same basic method of basket making for thousands of years. Baskets dating back to 6,000 B.C. have been found in this region.

- Some of the tribes in this area carved *Kachina* dolls. These dolls were beautifully decorated and symbolized spirits.

- One of the most famous Indians of the Southwest was the Apache, Cochise. For many years he and a small band of warriors terrorized settlers and others who entered their territory. They fought a bloody war with U.S. federal troops. Cochise and his men finally surrendered in 1872.

- One of the most famous Southwest Native Americans is Manuelito. This Navajo war chief led his people in fighting the efforts of the U.S. government to relocate them to New Mexico.

- Perhaps the most famous Indian of this region was Geronimo. Born in 1829 he led numerous raids against Mexicans and Americans. Apache chiefs relied on his wisdom. He died in 1909 as a prisoner of war.

- There were probably more battles fought between the Indians of the Southwest and the U.S. government than in any other Indian region.

- From 1849 to 1886 the Apache Indians of the Southwest fought a series of battles against the U.S. government in what is called the Apache Wars.

- The Navajo Indians of the Southwest have the largest Indian reservation in the U.S. It covers over seventeen million acres in New Mexico, Utah, and Arizona and is larger than some U.S. states.

- The Southwest Indian region is home to the largest Indian tribe in the U.S., the Navajo.

- Incredible Indian archaeological sites can be found throughout the southwest United States. Northern Arizona, near Flagstaff and Sedona in particular, is known for many ancient cliff dwellings and pueblo sites. This includes the ruins of Tuzigoot which is an amazing hill top pueblo built between 1125 and 1400 AD.

courses and parks, all dependent on imported water for irrigation. In spite of the increasing development of dams, reservoirs, and canals, the lack of water has remained a severe limitation to agricultural, urban, and industrial expansion and is sure to remain an important and controversial issue in the future.

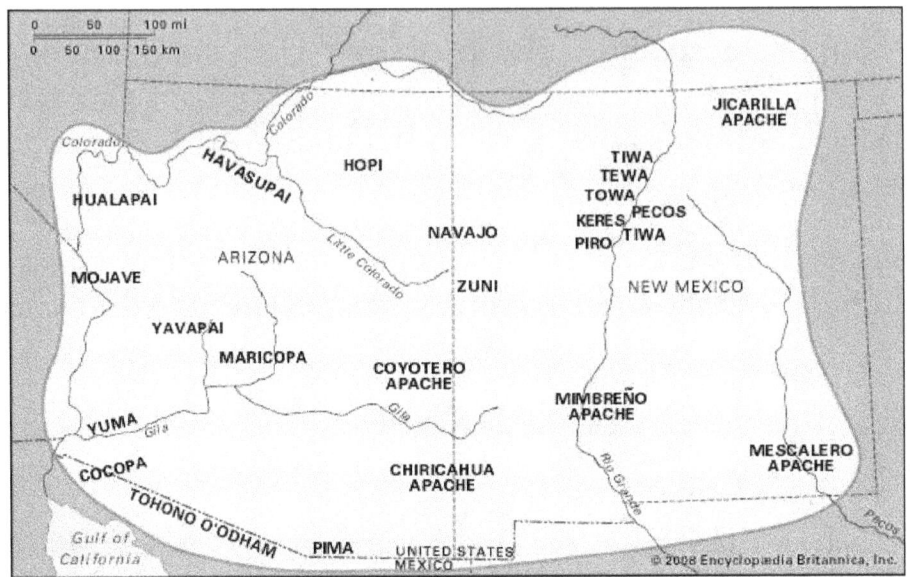

Fig. 69 Southwest Indian Tribes

The Indians of the region accumulated a rich natural lore during the thousands of years of their adaptation to the desert environment, but it was left to Francisco Vázquez de Coronado and other 16th-century Spanish explorers to provide the first written descriptions of the region, particularly of the southwestern portion. Although Stephen H. Long never saw the true North American Desert, his depiction of the "Great American Desert" fired the American public's imagination. John C. Frémont's mapping of the region in the 1840s foreshadowed a host of reports, often generated by the huge land grants made to railroads and land companies and written by 19th-century surveyor-engineers. In 1878 the geologist John Wesley Powell made a significant report on the arid West, accurately forecasting the detrimental consequences of imposing on arid regions ways of life more appropriate to humid lands. More diversified studies followed—the first arid-lands research laboratory was founded at Tucson, Arizona in 1903—and contemporary studies have included the important International Biological Program of ecological investigation.

The Southwest culture area **(Side Bar CC)** is located between the Rocky Mountains and the Mexican Sierra Madre. The Continental Divide separates the landscape into the watersheds of two great river systems: the Colorado–Gila–San Juan, in the west, and the Rio Grande–Pecos, in the east. The environment is arid, with some areas averaging less than 4 inches of precipitation each year; droughts are common. Despite its low moisture content, coarse texture, and occasional salty patches, the soil of most of the Southwest is relatively fertile.

The distribution of resources in the region is determined more by elevation than by latitude. The predominant landscape feature in the north is the Colorado Plateau, a cool, arid plain into which the Colorado and Rio Grande systems have carved deep canyons. Precipitation tends to be greater at the plateau's higher elevations, which support scrub and piñon-juniper woodland, rattlesnakes, rabbits, coyotes, bobcats, and mule deer. At lower elevations the plateau also supports grasses and antelope. To the south the river systems descend from the plateau, and canyons, mesas, and steep escarpments give way to a basin and range system. River valleys here support clusters of cottonwood, willow, mesquite, and sycamore trees, and mule deer, fish, and waterfowl. The areas away from the rivers are characterized by desert flora and fauna, including mesquite, creosote bush, cactus, yucca, small mammals, and reptiles.

The people of the Cochise culture **(Side Bar DD)** were among the earliest residents of the Southwest. A desert-adapted hunting and gathering culture whose diet emphasized plant foods and small game, this group lived in the region as early as *c.* 7000 BCE

Side Bar CC The Southwest Culture Area

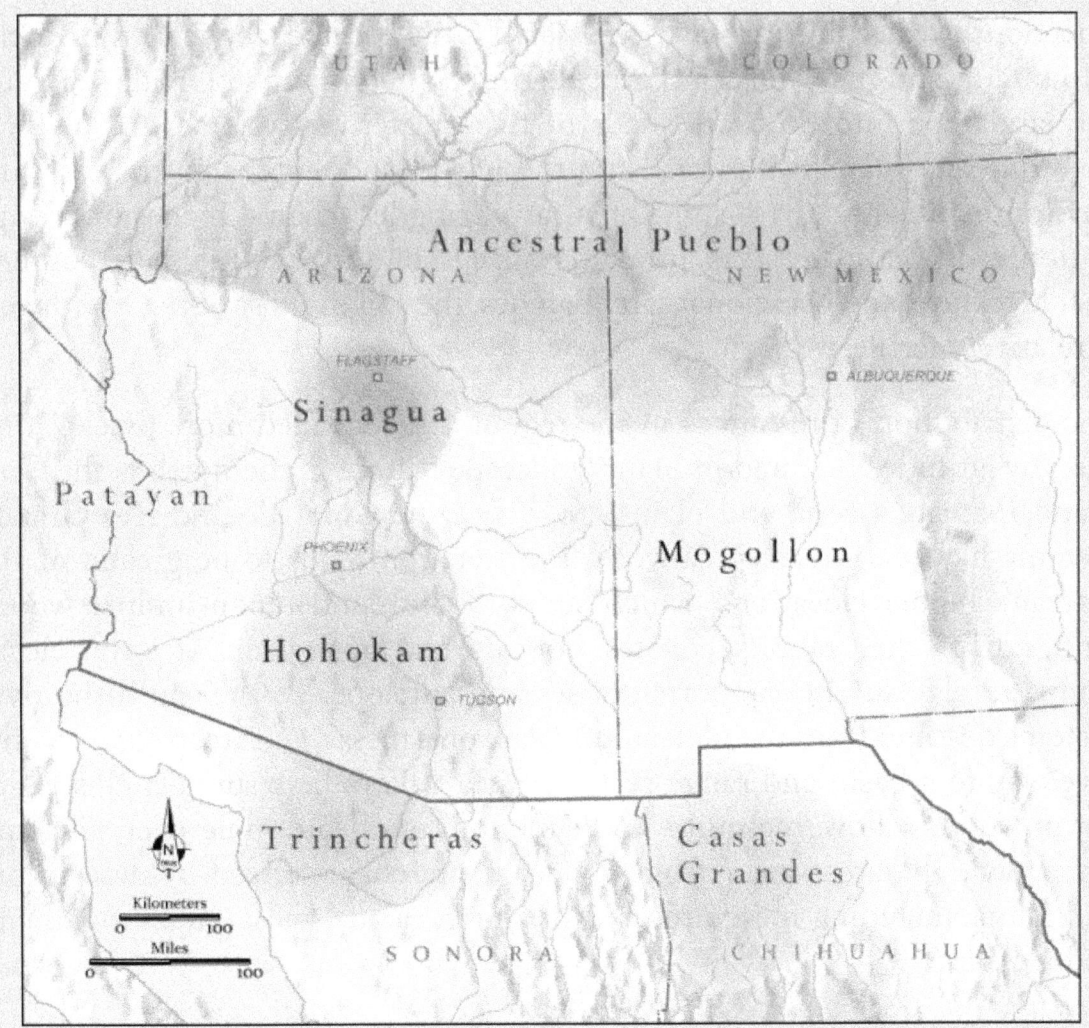

The Greater Southwest encompasses a broad area, including Arizona, New Mexico, southern Colorado, southern Utah, and far western Texas, as well as the northwest Mexican states of Chihuahua and Sonora. People lived in this arid to semi-arid landscape for more than 13,000 years before Europeans arrived, a period archaeologists now call the "precontact" or "prehispanic" era, though some still refer to "prehistory" and "prehistoric" sites or objects.

The precontact Southwest was a diverse cultural landscape inhabited by groups who probably spoke many different languages and saw themselves as distinct peoples. They made a living through hunting, collecting wild plants, and farming corn, beans, squash, and a variety of other crops. Peak population in the precontact era was probably almost 200,000 people.

On the most general level, archaeologists seek to understand how we have come to be who we are, collectively, as human beings living in societies. The ultimate question Southwest archaeologists are asking is, how did people survive, thrive, and solve the problems of living in this rugged and arid land for millennia?

By about 2,000 years ago, or perhaps even a bit earlier, there were clear regional differences across the Southwest. Major culture areas in the U.S. Southwest include the Ancestral Pueblo, the Mogollon, and the Hohokam. All of these groups were settled farmers, but there are key differences among them. Other archaeological culture areas in the Greater Southwest include Sinagua, Patayan, Trincheras, and Casa Grandes.

> **Side Bar DD The Cochise Culture**
>
> In the southeast region of Arizona, the culture known as the Cochise Culture flourished from about 9000BP (Before Present) to 2100BP. Three distinct phases have been adopted in describing the transitions of the Cochise: Sulpher Springs, Chiricahua, and San Pedro. The first stage demonstrates the notion of big game hunting as the main form of subsistence. Such prehistoric creatures as the mammoth, horse, and camel were the primary prey. Projectile points found below kill sites, as well as percussion-flaked knives, scrapers, and choppers strongly suggest such a claim. As the culture continued to advance technologically, such artifacts as stemmed points, storage pits, and heavy mill stones lead archaeologists to believe that farming had become an influential factor in the subsistence of this culture. By the time of the San Pedro phase, small pit houses were being used as simple shelters for the Cochise peoples. It is believed that the San Pedro phase of the Cochise Culture evolved into the modern Mogollon tradition.

Farming became important for subsequent residents including the Ancestral Pueblo (Anasazi; about 100–1600), the Mogollon (about 200–1450), and the Hohokam (about 200–1400). These groups lived in permanent and semi-permanent settlements that they sometimes built near (or even on) sheltering cliffs; developed various forms of irrigation; grew crops of corn (maize), beans, and squash; and had complex social and ritual habits. It is believed that the Ancestral Pueblo were the ancestors of the modern Pueblo Indians, that the Hohokam were the ancestors of the Pima and Tohono O'odham (Papago), and that the Mogollon dispersed or joined other communities.

The Southwest was home to representatives from several North American Indian language families, including Hokan, Uto-Aztecan, Tanoan, Keresan, Kiowa-Tanoan, Penutian, and Athabaskan.

The Hokan-speaking Yuman peoples were the westernmost residents of the region; they lived in the river valleys and the higher elevations of the basin and range system there. The so-called River Yumans, including the Quechan (Yuma), Mojave, Cocopa, and Maricopa, resided on the Lower Colorado and the Gila River; their cultures combined some traditions of the Southwest culture area with others of the California Indians. The Upland Yumans, including the Havasupai, Hualapai, and Yavapai, lived on secondary and ephemeral streams in the western basins and ranges.

Two groups that spoke Uto-Aztecan languages resided in the southwestern portion of the culture area, near the border between the present-day states of Arizona (U.S.) and Sonora (Mexico). The Tohono O'odham were located west of the Santa Cruz River. The closely related Pima lived along the middle Gila River.

The Pueblo Indians were linguistically diverse. Those living along the Rio Grande and its tributaries are generally referred to as the eastern Pueblos, while those on the Colorado Plateau are assigned to the western division. The eastern group included the Keresan-speaking Zia, Santa Ana, San Felipe, Santo Domingo, and Cochiti, and representatives of three members of the Kiowa-Tanoan language family: the Tewa-speaking San Ildefonso, San Juan, Santa Clara, Tesuque, and Nambe; the Tiwa-speaking Isleta, Sandia, Taos, and Picuris; and the Towa-speaking Jemez. The western Pueblo tribes included the Hopi (Uto-Aztecan; also Hopi language), Hano (Tanoan), Zuni (Penutian), and Acoma and Laguna (Keresan).

The Navajo and the closely related Apache spoke Athabaskan languages. The Navajo lived on the Colorado Plateau near the Hopi villages. The Apache traditionally resided in the range and basin systems south of the plateau. The major Apache tribes included the Western Apache, Chiricahua, Mescalero, Jicarilla, Lipan, and Kiowa Apache. The Athabaskan-speaking groups migrated from northwestern North America to the Southwest and probably did not reach the area until sometime between 1100 and 1500 CE.

Natives of the South American Deserts

The desert has hosted various indigenous peoples in its past, as evidenced by cave paintings in the area. The earliest inhabitants of the desert known by name are those of the Tehuelche complex. Tehuelches **(Side Bar Q)** lived as hunter-gatherers and did not practice agriculture in lush valleys found in the desert. In the 18th and 19th centuries the northern part of the desert came under Mapuche influence during a process of **Araucanization**. Mapuches came to practice horse husbandry in the northern part of the Patagonian steppe. Mapuche tribes came to control trade across the desert and traded with the cities of southern Chile as well as Buenos Aires and the Cuyo Region.

Fig. 70 Tehuelches

The Mapuche People

In their cultural framework the Mapuche people ("people of the land"; *mapu* = land; *che* = people) show great diversity in their ways of communicating and relating to nature, making them specialists in the care and management of natural resources. Both their native language (Mapudungun) and the names of their communities reflect the vital connection between the people and their land. In Patagonia several Mapuche populations and their descendants live in areas around streams and lakes, which are used by the rural inhabitants to cover their basic consumption and personal hygiene needs. Nevertheless, fish resources appear not to be fully used, given that at the end of the 19th century the Mapuche people incorporated livestock breeding as central to their way of life and as an essential means of subsistence **(Figure 71)**.

Fig. 71 Mapuche House

As in the majority of American indigenous peoples' cosmologies, for Mapuche people all of nature is alive, populated by beings or entities they have social relationships with relations between humans and nature where the visible and invisible worlds overlap or intersect. For the Mapuche people, animals in particular have enormous relevance in the universe of meanings and are strongly connected with the different spheres of their reality. This includes subsistence relationships, their connection with forebears and their ancestral lines, the representation of their social and ritual organization and origin myths among others. Thus, animals are part of their oral tradition and, therefore, subject to processes of cultural transmission.

The Wayuu Tribe

The Wayuu Tribe, known as the people of the sun, sand and wind, arrived in La Guajira from the Amazon rainforest nearly 2000 years ago to escape hostile environments and find a new home. Since then, the Wayuus have battled the Spanish Conquistadores, the Colombian Government and, currently, climate change to keep their traditions alive. Contraband, conflicts, scarcity, exploitation, and misgovernments affected the daily life of the Wayuu tribes surviving their land.

Located on the northernmost tip of South America, the harsh and arid Guajira Peninsula straddles the border of Venezuela and Colombia. Until recently, it was rarely visited by outsiders, in part related to its Wild West reputation as a hub for trafficking in humans, drugs, and other items, and as the home of the strong-willed Wayuu.

For 500 years, the Wayuu people have resisted all who have come to take their land or resources, from Spanish settlers in search of pearls to English pirates looking for treasure. The discovery of coal, oil, salt and gas, however, has succeeded in altering the equation, and rapacious multinational energy companies now threaten not only La Guajira but also the culture and way of life of the Wayuu **(Figure 72)**.

Fig. 72 Piichi or Miichi, Wayúu houses

Atacama Desert People

The origins of Atacameño culture **(Side Bar EE)** can be traced back to 500 AD. The Tiwanaku people were the first known conquerors. At the start of the 15th century, the Atacameño were conquered by the Inca. Topa Inca Yupanqui (translated as "noble Inca accountant"), introduced a new social order, the Inca sun cult and various customs including coca leaves. The Inca regime constructed roads from the Salar de Atacama to what is now north east Argentina.

In 1535, the first Spanish conquistadors arrived in the area and it was finally annexed under Spanish control in 1556. In the 18th century, the Atacameño Tomás Paniri joined the uprisings led by the Peruvian Túpac Amaru II and the Bolivian Túpac Katari. In 1824, the region became part of Bolivia and in 1883 fell into Chilean hands. In 2007, the Atacameño population was estimated at 21,015 people.

> **Side Bar EE The Atacama**
>
> The **Atacama,** also called **Atacameño,** or **Cunza,** extinct South American Indian culture of the Andean desert oases of northern Chile and northwestern Argentina. The last surviving groups of the Atacama have been assimilated by Spanish and Aymara culture.

VI. Future of the Desert

Major changes are likely to be experienced in the arid and semi-arid lands in the next few decades. The most important changes will be induced by increasing human pressure of various kinds: increasing population, both in rural and urban contexts, continuing oil developments and larger numbers of ambitious water developments. Urban populations have profound impacts in semi-arid lands, which are all the more obvious for the absence of vegetation cover. Rural populations may be reaching the limits of cultivable land in many areas and this could, though not necessarily have impacts on soils and vegetation. These changes may or may not be serious enough to influence climate and so induce a real and perhaps lasting change in these environments.

A study and review of deserts were performed and published by Warren, Sud and Rozanov (1996) resulting in these predictions for the future of deserts. Three of the predictions are quite safe. First, there will be substantial demands for urban land of all sorts, for housing, aggregate abstraction, waste disposal and water storage, among other things. Second, the demand for arable land in semi-arid areas will rapidly reach saturation, and pressure thereafter will be relieved in places by increasing soil degradation, but in others by increasing intensification of agriculture. Third, if there is major de-vegetation, either brought on by greater pressure on resources from increasing population growth, or from some change in global climate, however provoked, then there may well be a feed-back in which the result will be reductions in local rainfall. The safest forecast is that the deserts and the areas close to them will experience substantial change in the next few decades.

According to a new study by University of Maryland scientists, the Sahara Desert has expanded by about 10 percent since 1920. The research is the first to assess century-scale changes to the boundaries of the largest desert in the world and suggests that other deserts could be expanding as well.

The Sahara is the largest warm-weather desert in the world, roughly equal in size to the **contiguous** United States. (The Arctic basin and the Antarctic continent, which are each about twice as large as the Sahara, also qualify as deserts because their low rates of precipitation.) As all deserts, the boundaries of the Sahara fluctuate with the seasons, expanding in the dry winter and contracting during the wetter summer.

"With this study, our priority was to document the long-term trends in rainfall and temperature in the Sahara. Our next step will be to look at what is driving these trends, for the Sahara and elsewhere," Thomas, a graduate student in atmospheric and oceanic science at the University of Maryland explained. "We have already started looking at seasonal temperature trends over North America, for example. Here, winters are getting warmer but summers are about the same. In Africa, it's the opposite—winters are holding steady but summers are getting warmer. So the stresses in Africa are already more severe."

The results of this study have far-reaching implications for the future of the Sahara, as well as other subtropical deserts around the world. As the world's population continues to grow, a reduction in arable land with adequate rainfall to support crops could have devastating consequences.

Closer to home, researchers from the University of Arizona have found invasive species add to fire risk in Sonoran ecosystem. Following unusually high temperatures around the end of May, smoke has been seen rising at many places in the Sonoran Desert, and fire warnings have been issued across the region.

Until the arrival of alien weeds, wildfires were not a problem in the region, which stretches from the southwestern United States to northern Mexico. The native vegetation is not dense enough to burn well; but thickly growing non-native grasses, which dry up in summer, cover the ground in a layer that spreads fire easily. The weeds have also become a serious threat to desert biodiversity, as they compete with native plants such as the saguaro cactus, which can take decades to grow back after a fire.

To make matters worse, a shrubby grass known as buffelgrass (*Pennisetum ciliare*) has become common in the desert since the 1960s, and is largely responsible for increasing wildfire problem of the region since then; but ecologists fear that another invading weed, Sahara mustard (*Brassica tournefortii*), could have an even more devastating effect. "Sahara mustard is the greatest threat to the Sonoran," says Mark Dimmit, a botanist and director of natural history at the Arizona-Sonoran Desert Museum near Tucson. "If nothing is done, it could turn the desert into a wasteland."

Earlier this year, the Arizona state government put buffelgrass on a list of prohibited species, which means planting and transporting the noxious plants and their seeds is banned. In the Tucson area, where a wildfire threatened suburban neighborhoods in 2003, attempts are under way to eradicate buffelgrass mechanically. The weed grows near roads and highways, and in patches on desert hills and slopes.

Control is more difficult with Sahara mustard, which spreads extensively across valley floors, roadsides, rocky hillsides and even sand dunes. Its deep roots are hard to remove mechanically, and there is no biological agent for its control. "It's everywhere now," says Dimmit. "We really don't know what to do."

To gauge the scale of the problem, the Arizona-Sonoran Desert Museum began training a team of 'citizen scientists'. These volunteers will be equipped with data sheets and digital cameras and are about to begin mapping the weeds' spread.

Ecologists warn the problem is about to get far worse. Unless urgent action is taken, they fear the uncontrolled spread of exotic weeds could trigger an ecological disaster in the area, as the frequency of fires rises dramatically.

Restoring desert ecosystems is challenged by extreme climates, dry soils, seed predation, herbivory, and generally slow rates of plant colonization and growth. Despite these difficulties, at least partial restoration of desert ecosystems is possible. There are examples where restoration techniques such as out-planting initiated ecosystem recovery and accomplished project objectives (Abella and Newton 2009). Failed projects have illustrated there is little room for error when implementing desert restoration techniques, underscoring the importance of using good practices, such as planting good-quality stock at appropriate times of the year. Future research in desert restoration may help improve restoration techniques, provide an understanding of under which conditions different techniques work best, and identify situations where restoration is most feasible and has the greatest probability of success.

Glossary

Aquifers – any geological formation containing or conducting ground water, especially one that supplies the water for wells and springs.

Araucanization – The process of expansion of the Mapudungun language and others elements of the Mapuche culture from their homeland Araucania into the plains of Patagonia.

Arborescent – treelike

Atmosphere – the combination of the gases that surround the earth.

Barchans and transverse dunes – represent the classic dune morphology, displaying a crescentic shape with crests aligned perpendicular to the prevailing wind direction and horns directed parallel to it.

Biome – a specific environment that is home to living things suited for that place and climate.

Contiguous – connecting without a break

Desert – any area in which few forms of life can exist because of lack of water, permanent frost, or absence of soil.

Desert pavement – The rock mantle in deserts protects the underlying material from deflation.

Diaspora – a population scattered across regions separate from its geographic place of origin.

Eolian deflation – zones of desert pavement, a sheet-like surface of rock fragments remaining after wind and water have removed the fine particles

Falkland Current – is a cold water current that flows northward along the Atlantic coast of Patagonia as far north as the mouth of the Río de la Plata. This current results from the movement of water from the West Wind Drift as it rounds Cape Horn.

Felsic lava – describes igneous rocks that are relatively rich in elements that form feldspar and quartz.

Fluvial deposits – are sediments deposited by the flowing water of a stream.

Germination – to begin to grow; sprout.

Homogeneous – with uniform structure or composition throughout.

Hydrosphere – the water on the surface of the earth

Indigenous – produced, growing, living, or occurring natively or naturally in a particular region or environment.

Isotherm – a line on a map or chart of the surface of the earth connecting points having the same temperature at a given time or the same mean temperature for a given period.

Keeled scales – refer to reptile scales that, rather than being smooth, have a ridge down the center that may or may not extend to the tip of the scale, making them rough to the touch.

Longitudinal seifs – long ridges of blown sand, often several miles long

Moisture content – amount of water vapor in the air

Pastoralists – are found in many variations throughout the world, generally where crop growing is difficult or impossible. As result, they are historically nomadic people who move with their herds.

pH – is the most common and trusted way to measure the acid or base level of a substance

Rain shadow zones – the downwind sides of mountains that receive limited rainfall.

Sedentary – not migratory, settled.

Silk Road – an ancient trade route that linked the Western world with the Middle East and Asia. It was a major conduit for trade between the Roman Empire and China and later between medieval European kingdoms and China.

Steppe – one of the vast usually level and treeless tracts in southeastern Europe or Asia

Substrate – the surface on or in which plants, algae, or certain animals, such as barnacles or clams, live or grow

Wadi – a shallow usually sharply defined depression in a desert region of southwestern Asia and northern Africa.

Xeric scrubland – a type of desert biome. The ground is made up of sand, grass blocks, and acacia leaves. There seems to be a fair number of small water lakes.

Side Bars

Side Bar A Major Deserts of the World

Side Bar B Wind Direction

Side Bar C Atmospheric circulation

Side Bar D Hot and Cold Desert Regions

Side Bar E Climate types under the Köppen climate classification

Side Bar F Rain Shadow

Side Bar G Man-made Desert

Side Bar H World Deserts

Side Bar I Movement of Sand Dune

Side Bar J Arctic Desert

Side Bar K The Syrian Desert

Side Bar L 10 Interesting Kalahari Desert Facts

Side Bar M Desert Pavement of the Mojave

Side Bar N The Joshua tree

Side Bar O The Chihuahuan Desert

Side Bar P Silk Roads

Side Bar Q 15 Facts about the Mongolian Gobi Desert

Side Bar R Alashan Plateau semi-desert map

Side Bar S Takla Makan Desert map

Side Bar T More about the Silk Road

Side Bar U About Desert Plants

Side Bar V Fun Facts about the thorny devil

Side Bar W Berbers in North Africa

Side Bar X The Kabyle People

Side Bar Y The Blue Men

Side Bar Z The Bedouin

Side Bar AA The Beja People

Side Bar BB Facts about Southwest American Indian Tribes

Side Bar CC The Southwest Culture Area

Side Bar DD The Cochise Culture

Side Bar EE The Atacama

List of Illustrations

List of Figures:
Fig. 1 Hot deserts of the world
Fig. 2 World's 10 largest deserts.
Fig. 3 Desertification
Fig. 4 Planting a tree
Fig. 5 Map of the Sahara Desert
Fig. 6 Map of Antarctica
Fig. 7 Undulating Dune
Fig. 8 Polar Desert – Antarctica
Fig, 9   Sand dunes in the Sahara, Morocco
Fig, 10 Ergs or seas of sand
Fig. 11 Barchans and transverse dune
Fig. 12 View looking upward to top of a longitudinal dune
Fig. 13 Map of the Arabian Desert
Fig. 14 The Arabian Desert
Fig. 15 The Syrian Desert
Fig. 16 The Kalahari Desert
Fig. 17 The four North American deserts
Fig. 18 The Great Basin Desert
Fig. 19 Map of the Mohave Desert

Fig. 20 Map of the Chihuahuan Desert
Fig. 21 Map of the Sonoran Desert
Fig. 22 The Sonoran Desert Landscape
Fig. 23 Sonoran Desert Vegetative Regions
Fig. 24 Atacama Desert
Fig. 25 The Patagonian Desert
Fig. 26 Atacama Desert 2
Fig. 27 The La Guajira Desert
Fig. 28 Gobi Desert map
Fig. 29 Rain Shadow Effect
Fig. 30 Eastern Gobi Desert steppe
Fig. 31 Alashan Plateau semi-desert
Fig. 32 Gobi Lakes Valley desert steppe
Fig. 33 Dzungarian Basin semi desert
Fig. 34 Central Tian Shan Mountains
Fig. 35 Karakum Desert
Fig. 36 Darvaza Gas Crater
Fig. 37 Takla Makan Desert
Fig. 38 The Gobi Desert
Fig. 39 Desert of Lop
Fig. 40 The Silk Road
Fig. 41 Australia - 10 Deserts
Fig. 42 The Great Victoria Desert
Fig. 43 Great Sandy Desert
Fig. 44 Ergs of the Great Sandy Desert
Fig. 45 the Kata Tjuta domes
Fig. 46 Ayres Rock
Fig. 47 Wolfe Creek Meteorite Crater
Fig. 48 desert greasewood

Fig. 49 African Peyote
Fig. 50 Sahara lovegrass
Fig. 51 date palm tree
Fig. 52 mesquite-tree
Fig. 53 Palo Verde tree
Fig. 54 Fennec Fox
Fig. 55 Addux antelope
Fig. 56 Deathstalker scorpion
Fig. 57 Camel
Fig. 58 thorny devil
Fig. 59 Rockhopper penguin
Fig. 60 Sand cat
Fig. 61 Saharan horned viper
Fig. 62 The mazaalai
Fig. 63 Baer's pochard
Fig. 64 Mongolian ground jay
Fig. 65 Pallas's sandgrouse
Fig. 66 Tuareg woman
Fig. 67 Saans People
Fig. 68 Aboriginal woman
Fig. 69 Southwest Indian Tribes
Fig. 70 Tehuelches
Fig. 71 Mapuche House
Fig. 72 Piichi or Miichi, Wayúu houses

Illustration Credits

BirdLife International (2023) Species factsheet: *Aythya baeri*. Downloaded from http://www.birdlife.org on 15/02/2023

Koppen_World_Map_Hi-Res.png: Peel, M. C., Finlayson, B. L., and McMahon, T. A.(University of Melbourne)derivative work: Me ne frego (talk) - Koppen_World_Map_Hi-Res.png, CC BY-SA 3.0,

https://commons.wikimedia.org/w/index.php?curid=14783182

https://en.wikipedia.org/wiki/Desert_climate#/media/File:Koppen_World_Map_BWh.png

https://www.desertusa.com/flora/palo-verde-tree.html

https://www.britannica.com/animal/addax-antelope

https://www.scorpionworlds.com/deathstalker-scorpion/

https://www.oddizzi.com/teachers/explore-the-world/physical-features/ecosystems/deserts/what-can-you-find/animals/

https://en.wikipedia.org/wiki/Cerastes_cerastes

https://www.britannica.com/place/Arabian-Desert/Climate

https://www.touristsecrets.com/destinations/ultimate-guide-to-the-lonely-kalahari-desert-south-africa/

https://www.britannica.com/place/Sahara-desert-Africa

https://www.desertmuseum.org/books/nhsd_northamerica.php

https://www.nps.gov/moja/planyourvisit/cima-road.htm

https://www.desertusa.com/chihuahuan-desert.html

http://museum2.utep.edu/chih/chihdes.htm

https://en.wikipedia.org/wiki/Patagonian_Desert

https://www.worldatlas.com/articles/the-major-deserts-of-south-america.html

https://www.fodors.com/world/south-america/colombia/experiences/news/11-incredible-photos-of-colombias-guajira-desert

https://www.amicusmongolia.com/15-facts-about-mongolian-gobi-desert.

https://www.britannica.com/place/Takla-Makan-Desert

https://10deserts.org/desert/great-victoria-desert/

https://en.wikipedia.org/wiki/Great_Sandy_Desert

https://www.britannica.com/place/Great-Victoria-Desert

https://www.britannica.com/place/Great-Sandy-Desert

https://www.australia.com/en/places/alice-springs-and-surrounds/guide-to-kata-tjuta.html

https://www.bhg.com/gardening/plant-dictionary/tree/date-palm/

https://davesgarden.com/guides/articles/view/2762

https://en.wikipedia.org/wiki/Camel

https://www.nasa.gov/audience/forstudents/k-4/stories/nasa-knows/what-is-antarctica-k4.html

https://www.iwp.edu/active-measures/2019/09/08/mexican-transnational-criminal-organizations-exploitation-of-the-sonoran-desert-and-the-tohono-oodham-nation/

https://www.nationsonline.org/oneworld/map/syria-topographic-map.htm

https://www.mitchellmuseum.org/education/documents/5SouthwestLessonPlanFINAwithheadersL.pdf

https://awasi.com/blog/the-tehuelches-indians-the-native-tribes-of-patagonia-southern-chile/

https://theculturetrip.com/south-america/chile/articles/a-brief-history-of-chiles-indigenous-mapuche-people/

https://www.livescience.com/64752-atacama-desert.html

https://www.britannica.com/topic/Bedouin

https://joshuaproject.net/people_groups/12399/AG

https://www.archaeologysouthwest.org/ancient-cultures/

https://en.wikipedia.org/wiki/Desert_climate#/media/File:BW_climate.png

https://www.un.org/en/observances/desertification-day

https//www.sciencedirect.com › topics › earth-and-planetary-sciences › barchan

https://en.wikipedia.org/wiki/Horse_latitudes#/media/File:Atmospheric_circulation.svg

http://mojavedesert.net/description.html

https://www.worldatlas.com/articles/where-is-the-lop-desert.html

https://www.fs.usda.gov/database/feis/plants/shrub/lartri/all.html

https://www.bhg.com/gardening/plant-dictionary/tree/date-palm/

https://theecologist.org/2016/jul/01/radioactive-waste-and-nuclear-war-australias-aboriginal-people

Sources

Abella, S.R. and A.C. Newton. 2009. A systematic review of species performance and treatment effectiveness for revegetation in the Mojave Desert, USA. Pages 45-74 *In*: A. Fernandez-Bernal and M.A. De La Rosa (editors). Arid environments and wind erosion. Nova Science Publishers, Inc., Hauppauge, NY

Anonymous 2019.The Arawak: The History and Legacy of the Indigenous Natives in South America and the Caribbean. Charles River Editors, Amazon.

Erickson, Winston P. 2003. Sharing the Desert: The Tohono O'odham in History. University of Arizona Press, Tucson, AZ

https://www.bbc.com/bitesize/guides/zpnq6fr/revision/4

https://www.britannica.com/topic/list-of-deserts-1854209

https://www.britannica.com/topic/Beja-people

https://www.britannica.com/animal/addax-antelope

https://sciencing.com/do-plants-animals-adapt-desert-6516007.html

https://en.wikipedia.org/wiki/Desert_climate

https://www.oddizzi.com/teachers/explore-the-world/physical-features/ecosystems/deserts/what-can-you-find/animals/

https://www.scorpionworlds.com/deathstalker-scorpion/

https://en.wikipedia.org/wiki/Camel

https://en.wikipedia.org/wiki/Cerastes_cerastes

http://www.eniscuola.net/en/argomento/desert/man-and-desert/the-desert-peoples/

https://en.wikipedia.org/wiki/Berbers

https://en.wikipedia.org/wiki/Bedouin

https://en.wikipedia.org/wiki/Beja_people

https://en.wikipedia.org/wiki/San_people

https://en.wikipedia.org/wiki/Aboriginal_Australians

https://pubs.usgs.gov/gip/deserts/types/

https://www.worldatlas.com/articles/10-largest-deserts-in-the-world.html

https://www.insider.com/photos-of-gates-of-hell-fire-crater-turkmenistan

https://www.livescience.com/23140-sahara-desert.html

http://www.eyesonafrica.net/Articles/deserts-africa.htm

https://www.safaribookings.com/blog/10-interesting-kalahari-desert-facts

https://www.touristsecrets.com/destinations/ultimate-guide-to-the-lonely-kalahari-desert-south-africa/

https://www.britannica.com/place/Sahara-desert-Africa

https://www.desertmuseum.org/books/nhsd_northamerica.php

https://en.wikipedia.org/wiki/Patagonian_Desert

https://www.worldatlas.com/articles/the-major-deserts-of-south-america.html

https://www.amicusmongolia.com/15-facts-about-mongolian-gobi-desert.

https://www.insider.com/photos-of-gates-of-hell-fire-crater-turkmenistan

https://www.britannica.com/place/Takla-Makan-Desert

https://en.wikipedia.org/wiki/Great_Victoria_Desert#Environment

https://10deserts.org/desert/great-victoria-desert/

https://en.wikipedia.org/wiki/Deserts_of_Australia

https://en.wikipedia.org/wiki/Great_Victoria_Desert

https://en.wikipedia.org/wiki/Great_Sandy_Desert

https://www.desertusa.com/du_great-sandy.html

https://www.britannica.com/place/North-American-Desert/The-people-and-economy

https://www.britannica.com/topic/Southwest-Indian

https://www.ncbi.nlm.nih.gov/pmc/articles/PMC5143445/

https://www.thestoryinstitute.com/wayuu

https://www.desertusa.com/thingstodo/du_safetytips.html

https://en.wikipedia.org/wiki/Syrian_Desert

https://www.britannica.com/place/Syrian-Desert

https://www.latlong.net/place/syrian-desert-syria-1357.html

https://www.britannica.com/place/Mongolia/The-northern-intermontane-basins#ref394656

https://awasi.com/blog/the-tehuelches-indians-the-native-tribes-of-patagonia-southern-chile/

https://theculturetrip.com/south-america/chile/articles/a-brief-history-of-chiles-indigenous-mapuche-people/

https://biomesoplenty.fandom.com/wiki/Xeric_Shrubland

https://www.britannica.com/topic/Silk-Road-trade-route

https://www.researchgate.net/publication/341111257_Nesting_Behavior_of_the_MongolianGround_Jay_Podoces_hendersoni_in_the_Gobi_Desert_of_Southern_Mongolia

https://pubs.usgs.gov/gip/deserts/features/

https://saniealieva.wordpress.com/about-desert-plants/

https://doi.org/10.1093/acrefore/9780190277734.013.105

https://www.krugerpark.co.za/africa_bushmen.html

Opportunities to Improve Soil and Water Quality *In*: National Research Council. 1993. Soil and Water Quality: An Agenda for Agriculture. Washington, DC: The National Academies Press. DOI: 10.17226/2132

Pye, Kenneth and Tsoar, Haim. 2009. Page 155 *In;* Aeolian Sand and Sand Dunes. Springer-Verlag, Berlin, Germany

Schiermeier, Q. 2005. Pall hangs over desert's future as alien weeds fuel wildfires. Nature 435: 724.

Thomas, Natalie and Sumant Nigam. 2018. Twentieth-Century Climate Change over Africa: Seasonal Hydroclimate Trends and Sahara Desert Expansion. Journal of Climate 31 (9): 3349 DOI: 10.1175/JCLI-D-17-0187.1

Tumendemberel, Odbayar, Tebbenkamp, Joel M., Zedrosser, Andreas, Proctor, Michael F., Blomberg, Erik J., Morin, Dana J., Rosell, Frank, Reynolds, Harry V., Adams, Jennifer R., Waits, Lisette P. 2021. Long-term monitoring using DNA sampling reveals the dire demographic status of the critically endangered Gobi bear. Ecosphere 12(8). DOI:10.1002/ecs2.3696

Warren, A., Y.C. Sud and B. Rozanov (the late). 1996. The future of deserts. Journal of Arid Environments 32(1):75-89.

Yakan, Muḥammad Z. 1999. Almanac of African Peoples and Nations. Routledge, Abingdon, UK

About the Author

Mary Jo Nickum is a retired librarian, teacher, and an award-winning writer and editor. She is also a biologist, specializing in fish and other aquatic as well as terrestrial life. She enjoys writing about biological subjects for kids. She has won Excellence in Craft awards from the Outdoor Writers Association of America (OWAA) for her books and magazine articles. Visit her website www.asktheanimallady.com for more about animals.

www.ingramcontent.com/pod-product-compliance
Lightning Source LLC
Chambersburg PA
CBHW081157020426
42333CB00020B/2536